History of New Zealand

A Captivating Guide to the History of the Land of the Long White Cloud, from the Polynesians Through the Māori Musket Wars to the Present

© Copyright 2023 - All rights reserved.

The content contained within this book may not be reproduced, duplicated, or transmitted without direct written permission from the author or the publisher.

Under no circumstances will any blame or legal responsibility be held against the publisher, or author, for any damages, reparation, or monetary loss due to the information contained within this book, either directly or indirectly.

<u>Legal Notice:</u>

This book is copyright protected. It is only for personal use. You cannot amend, distribute, sell, use, quote, or paraphrase any part, or the content within this book, without the consent of the author or publisher.

<u>Disclaimer Notice:</u>

Please note the information contained within this document is for educational and entertainment purposes only. All effort has been executed to present accurate, up-to-date, reliable, and complete information. No warranties of any kind are declared or implied. Readers acknowledge that the author is not engaging in the rendering of legal, financial, medical, or professional advice. The content within this book has been derived from various sources. Please consult a licensed professional before attempting any techniques outlined in this book.

By reading this document, the reader agrees that under no circumstances is the author responsible for any losses, direct or indirect, that are incurred as a result of the use of the information contained within this document, including, but not limited to, errors, omissions, or inaccuracies.

Free Bonus from Captivating History (Available for a Limited time)

Hi History Lovers!

Now you have a chance to join our exclusive history list so you can get your first history ebook for free as well as discounts and a potential to get more history books for free! Simply visit the link below to join.

Captivatinghistory.com/ebook

Also, make sure to follow us on Facebook, Twitter and Youtube by searching for Captivating History.

Table of Contents

INTRODUCTION 1
CHAPTER 1 - PREHISTORIC NEW ZEALAND AND ITS FIRST HUMANS (THE BEGINNING–1300) 3
CHAPTER 2 - NEW ZEALAND AND ITS PEOPLE BEFORE EUROPEAN CONTACT (1300-1642) 10
CHAPTER 3 - THE DUTCH DISCOVERY OF NEW ZEALAND, MAPMAKING, AND ITS NAMING (1600-1642) 25
CHAPTER 4 - FIRST EUROPEAN CONTACT WITH THE MĀORI AND TASMAN'S JOURNEYS (1642-1769) 29
CHAPTER 5 - JAMES COOK AND THE BRITISH CLAIM TO NEW ZEALAND (1769-1780) 36
CHAPTER 6 - FRENCH EXPLORERS' CONTACTS WITH NEW ZEALAND BEFORE SETTLEMENT AND THE MUSKET WARS (1770-1830) 47
CHAPTER 7 - THE FIRST BRITISH COLONIZATION EFFORTS IN NEW ZEALAND (1820-1842) 59
CHAPTER 8 - THE FIRST DECADES OF BRITISH SETTLEMENT 68
CHAPTER 9 - NEW ZEALAND IN THE 20TH CENTURY 87
CHAPTER 10 - NEW ZEALAND TODAY (2000-PRESENT) 100
CONCLUSION 104
HERE'S ANOTHER BOOK BY CAPTIVATING HISTORY THAT YOU MIGHT LIKE 106
FREE BONUS FROM CAPTIVATING HISTORY (AVAILABLE FOR A LIMITED TIME) 107
BIBLIOGRAPHY 108

Introduction

In the 13th century, when Polynesian explorers finally reached New Zealand, all of Earth's other large territories with livable conditions had been discovered and inhabited, making the two large islands in the Pacific Ocean that would become known as New Zealand the newest livable land in the world. Like most of the Pacific Islands, New Zealand has a diverse landscape ranging from volcanoes and snowcapped mountains to sandy beaches. Lying on the edge of two tectonic plates, New Zealand is an extremely volatile place to live (much like the other islands the Polynesians came from and discovered). Yet the explorers who discovered New Zealand decided to settle. They became known as the Māori.

New Zealand was ignored not only by Asian explorers for millennia but also by Europeans, who would not discover New Zealand until the 17th century. Unimpressed with New Zealand's inconvenient sailing routes, seemingly infertile land, and hostile people, it would take another 100 years for Europeans to revisit the islands and another century after that to begin colonizing. This meant that the Māori people, the most modern community to claim uninhabited land, also had a long period of mostly uninterrupted development. This might explain why the Māori were more involved in the European settlement process in New Zealand than natives in most other countries. Over 500 Māori chiefs signed the Treaty of Waitangi in 1840, which allowed England to establish a colony in New Zealand so long as Māori rights were respected.

Colonization was slow in the North Island as the Māori fought their bloody Musket Wars. However, the South Island quickly developed when gold was discovered in Otago in 1860. After gradual economic growth, mostly involving agriculture, New Zealand modernized faster than most nations; for example, it was the first country to grant women suffrage in 1893 and offer state pensions in 1898 and state housing in 1937. New Zealand gained independence in 1907, becoming a dominion of Great Britain; however, it remained closely tied economically, politically, and socially to its monarchy. Despite its connection to England, New Zealand developed a distinct culture in the 20th century, mostly surrounding rugby, racing, drinking, and its strong and capable military. The world recognized New Zealand's combat abilities after the country's participation in the South African War, World War I and II, and the Korean and Vietnam Wars. Today, the nation still has a rather small population of just over five million, with the majority concentrated in Auckland, its largest city.

Chapter 1 – Prehistoric New Zealand and Its First Humans (The Beginning–1300)

New Zealand's Late Human Occupancy

During Europe's intense exploration and colonization battles, few territories were left untouched. Most discovered territories had been claimed by the end of the 17th century, and the European superpowers had begun settling into their new colonies. However, some territories were not considered worth colonizing, whether due to seemingly hostile populations, unsafe sailing routes, or unprofitable or unfertile lands. Despite being discovered in the 17th century and having been visited by various European nations, New Zealand would not be colonized until the 19th century. While most territories deemed not worth colonizing still had massive indigenous populations that had been living on the lands for millennia, this was not the case for New Zealand. Even though New Zealand's closest neighbor, Australia, is believed to have been inhabited for more than 60,000 years, New Zealand's occupancy did not begin until the 13th century. This makes New Zealand one of the last (if not the last) large landmass with tolerable human conditions to be inhabited. Why did New Zealand's discovery, occupancy, and colonization take so long, and what was the territory like before human's late arrival?

New Zealand Before Human Occupancy

Unlike other developed nations that have invested decades and millions of dollars into uncovering their prehistoric pasts, New Zealand lagged rather far behind in archeological discoveries. That is, until the 1970s, when Joan Wiffen decided to further investigate geological maps that referenced reptilian bones in Hawke's Bay, on New Zealand's North Island. In 1975, Wiffen and her family discovered a dinosaur tail, disproving the long-held belief that New Zealand's isolation prevented it from being the home of dinosaurs and other prehistoric creatures. Archaeology still has a long way to go in New Zealand before we can truly understand the territory's ancient history, specifically concerning dinosaurs, as only four archaeological sites have uncovered dinosaur bones in New Zealand. While New Zealanders were slow to discover dinosaur bones, plenty of other fossils have been discovered in New Zealand that help us understand the fauna living on the islands today.

In the 1990s, bones of the extinct giant penguin, kairuku grebneffi (which was over four feet tall), were discovered in New Zealand. Two decades later, a group of school children in Otago discovered fossils of another giant penguin, the waewaeroa, which was likely at least half a foot taller than the largest previously-discovered penguins in New Zealand.

While emperor penguins (some of the world's largest penguins) do live in New Zealand, these prehistoric penguins would have been about double the height and weight of modern emperor penguins, so likely around 100 pounds. These newer fossils dated to around 27.3 and 34.6 million years old, which would have been about the time the Otago region, where they were discovered, was completely flooded. Other than dinosaurs, these prehistoric penguins are some of the oldest creatures that roamed New Zealand. Since the arrival of humans in New Zealand, the population of birds is believed to have halved. And, while archeologists have spent decades discovering and identifying fossils, it will likely take many more decades to get a better picture of the hundreds of New Zealander birds that went extinct.

One example of a species of bird that went extinct directly due to human occupation in New Zealand is the moa, which at its smallest was the size of a typical turkey and at its largest could weigh over 500 pounds and be nearly twelve feet tall. Yet, despite the size difference, these massive birds went instinct only two centuries after humans arrived in

New Zealand.

Reconstruction of a moa.
https://commons.wikimedia.org/wiki/File:Moa_mock_hunt.jpg

Since birds had no real predators until the arrival of humans, many New Zealand birds never needed to learn how to fly, which can be seen in penguins and the iconic kiwi bird that has come to represent modern-day New Zealand. Moas were also flightless birds, which explains how humans could drive them to extinction so quickly. Other iconic New Zealand birds that went extinct after the arrival of humans include prehistoric versions of owls, ducks, swans, and geese. When Europeans first arrived in New Zealand, scientific reports really only spoke of birds, helping us to understand how truly impactful they were on the early history of New Zealand.

Interestingly, it seems New Zealand was late to not only human occupation but also land mammal occupation, as the territories had few native land mammals. New Zealand did have a few species of bats and some mammalian sea creatures; however, other than some reptiles, New Zealand's prehistoric fauna is mostly defined by birds.

New Zealand's First People

As with most territories, the exact date of New Zealand's human occupation is extremely controversial and ever-changing as new evidence is discovered. However, the chances of archeological proof confirming the dates of human arrival is unlikely due to the Kaharoa eruption of the

Mount Tarawera volcano around 1314. Although archeologists are still working to uncover details about exactly why Mount Tarawera erupted, some scientists believe that this natural disaster was one of the earliest examples of mass human destruction in New Zealand—a pattern that would continue, as made obvious by the islands' mass bird extinction.

It is now commonly believed that the first people in New Zealand were Polynesians, who would become known as the Māori. However, Europeans originally believed that another people group predated the arrival of the Polynesians, a theory that has been revisited many times in recent history. Some theorists believe the first people in New Zealand were actually from Melanesia, the Oceanic region next to Polynesia. Others believe it may have been Eastern Asians or even Europeans who first visited New Zealand. These theories have little backing and are often used to squash the Māori people's claim to the land. Most evidence supports the theory that Polynesians were New Zealand's first people; therefore, this is the most commonly-accepted origin story by historians.

Arrival of the Polynesians

New Zealand has been two islands for the past twenty-five million years. Originally all of New Zealand was under the ocean. But, millions of years ago, as the Australian and the Pacific tectonic plates shifted, rocks were pushed out of the ocean, forming New Zealand's mountainous, rocky landscape. Through fossils, we can understand how New Zealand's land has changed over millions of years, and those shifts never resulted in a land bridge of any kind (unlike Australia, whose indigenous people could walk now-flooded land bridges to reach it). While this would explain why New Zealand took so long to be inhabited by humans, it doesn't explain how the humans finally arrived. While a lot of controversy surrounds exactly how the Polynesians reached New Zealand across a massive ocean, the most logical and widely-accepted answer is that they must have used some sort of boat.

Historians have long been fascinated by how certain plants, animals, tools, and structures made it so far away from their native homes before the advancement of transit. One item whose scattering is a long-held scientific mystery is the sweet potato. Despite being native to South America, radiocarbon dating has proven that sweet potatoes began appearing in Polynesia around the 11th century. Until recently, it was believed that sweet potato seeds must've been transported somehow by nature. Perhaps they were stuck in driftwood, seaweed, or in the stomach of birds that somehow made it all the way from sweet potatoes' native land of Ecuador and Peru to the Polynesian islands. While this may be true, archeologists began looking into the possibility that over a millennia ago, Polynesians had far more advanced boats and seafaring skills than we could imagine. According to Patrick Kirch, an archeologist at the University of Berkeley, "There's a lot of evidence accumulating over the last ten years that the Polynesians made landfall in South America. We think they had sophisticated, double-hulled canoes—like very large catamarans—which could carry 80 or more people and be out to sea for months" (Kirch, 2017). This claim is furthered by the fact that the remains of chickens were also discovered in South America before the arrival of the Europeans. Chickens are native to China; they then spread throughout Asia and were found in South America and Hawaii around 800 years ago. Considering that the Hawaiian Islands were also occupied by the Polynesians by the 12th century, the theory that Polynesians sailed the oceans in more-than-capable ships and could have reached New Zealand is not far-fetched.

Interestingly, sweet potatoes would also indicate approximately when Polynesians arrived in New Zealand, as the first yams were present around the 13th century. Chicken bones, on the other hand, can only be dated as far back as the 18th century in New Zealand. As in their supposed journey to South America and definite journey to Hawaii, the well-traveled Polynesians managed to weather the dangerous waters that kept humans away for so long and reach New Zealand.

Along with the sweet potato, it is believed that the first humans brought many new varieties of plants and New Zealand's first land mammals, notably dogs and rats. Dogs were actually very crucial in helping historians understand the settlement patterns of New Zealand's first humans. While very few human bones were discovered from the late 12th and early 13th centuries, an abundance of dog bones can be dated to that period. Dogs were very important to early humans, just as they are today, as they served as companions, hunters, guards—and food. Dogs' remains were also used by New Zealand's first humans to create all sorts of necessary items. For example, their bones were turned into fish hooks and their skins into cloaks. An entire book can be written on the interesting breeding and movement patterns of New Zealand's first dogs and what this says about the territory's first people. Genetic testing of New Zealand's dogs proves that most early dogs were related. This lack of diversity in their DNA demonstrates that one large group of people and dogs likely arrived in New Zealand and gradually spread and settled throughout the two islands.

How Māori People Differ from Polynesians

This pattern of a small group of Polynesians arriving on an island, spreading, settling, and reproducing is not just what occurred in New Zealand but in almost all the islands inhabited by people of Polynesian descent. During a new study conducted by the National Laboratory of Genomics for Biodiversity in Mexico, lead scientist Andres Moreno-Estrada gathered and tested genomes from twenty-one islands inhabited by Polynesian people. He discovered that, while some DNA was shared by all of these Pacific islanders, each island's inhabitants seemed to have their own rare genetics that differentiated the genomes of each island from one another. Most variants that appeared were not shared with the population of islands that were inhabited later, which led Moreno-Estrada and historians to believe that the Polynesian islands (including New Zealand) were first inhabited by very small founding populations. The fact that these genomes did not seem to spread from one island to another has led historians to assume the order the Pacific Islands were inhabited, which helps confirm New Zealand's habitation date. Since the DNA of indigenous people in New Zealand closely matched the ancient DNA collected, historians can also reliably confirm that the islands were not populated by future migrations but by one main immigration group. Thus, after years of breeding and isolation from other Polynesian people, the first people of New Zealand developed their own ethnic group and became known as the Māori.

The Māori's Archaic Period

Most modern historians divide the Māori's pre-European inhabitation of New Zealand into two periods, the first of which is the Archaic period. The Archaic phase is said to have lasted from the Polynesians' first arrival in New Zealand, estimated to be around 1280, until 1300. During these two decades, the Māori people explored the land and created small settlements of about 300 people, mostly along the coast—though there is evidence of a few small, less permanent settlements inland. Although the Polynesians began occupying New Zealand more recently than other territories' first people, very little is known, including the exact number of people who first arrived in New Zealand. By the first arrival of the Europeans in the mid-18th century, it is estimated there were around 100,000 Māori people in New Zealand. That said, the first Europeans to step foot in New Zealand stayed mostly around the coast, which means their estimation did not include any of the settlements further inland. Since historians approximate that the Polynesian canoes could hold around 100 people, and the Māori people seemed to arrive in one main immigration group, several ships would have had to travel together.

Although it may be far from accurate, this drawing (created by Dutch artist Isaack Gilsemans in 1642) may indicate the style of canoe used by the Māori. The sheer number of boats in the background also indicates the group traveling patterns of the early inhabitants of New Zealand.
https://commons.wikimedia.org/wiki/File:Gilsemans_1642.jpg

Very little is known about the Māori's Archaic period, but what is known is that the economy, diet, and lifestyle were extremely dependent on hunting. Based on what little remains can be uncovered from this time, the Archaic Māori population's diet it seems to have depended mostly on seals and moas. While there was also fishing and some agriculture, hunting was certainly the main food source, explaining the early Māori's nomadic lifestyles. Although the Polynesians were reliant on agriculture before immigrating to New Zealand, their new home had a totally different climate they would need to adjust to. Compared to their warm, tropical native lands, it was much cooler and more forested. This meant that many of the crops originally brought by the Polynesians to New Zealand, including the coconut, banana, and breadfruit, could not grow. Since the first people of New Zealand were mostly focused on surviving and exploring, there was little warring.

Chapter 2 – New Zealand and Its People Before European Contact (1300–1642)

The Māori's Classic Period

The second Māori period, known as the Classic period, is defined by historians as starting in 1300 and continuing until the arrival of the Europeans. This time, known as *Te Tipunga*, the Māori words for "The Growth," was much more turbulent and transformative than the Archaic period. This makes sense, considering it was about ten times longer. Overall, these two centuries are marked by change and development, not only in the people but also in the land they inhabited.

While much of New Zealand's change in landscape would be caused by human occupation, New Zealand is a land known for its potential for natural disasters. This is, of course, because the two islands are located in seismic zones. This means that New Zealand is prone to earthquakes, tsunamis, and volcanic eruptions. As mentioned earlier, New Zealand's first people dealt with the Kaharoa eruption of Mount Tarawera around 1314. This not only wiped out most of the settlements and evidence of the early human occupation but also likely killed thousands of people and drastically changed New Zealand's landscape. Although this volcanic eruption had especially dramatic effects, the Polynesian islands are known for their volcanoes, so the Māori people had experience dealing with them. The Pacific Islands are also prone to tsunamis, earthquakes, tropical storms, and forest fires, and these natural disasters seemed to be never-ending in the Māori's early years in New Zealand. It seemed as if there was nowhere safe to live in New Zealand. Coastal settlements were wrecked by tsunamis and floods, and inland settlements were subject to earthquakes and landslides.

Yet, despite the major events that seemed to define the Classic Māori period, the Māori people continued to spread out, populate the islands, and create permanent settlements. However, the people in the Chatham Islands would remain so isolated from the Māori who settled and spread out on New Zealand's main two islands that they would develop their own culture and ethnic group; they are known as the Moriori.

This map illustrates early Māori settlements before European contact and demonstrates how the Māori people spread out after their arrival. Not illustrated on the map is the first place the Māori people settled: the Chatham Islands.

(Created by author)

Diet of the Classic Māori

While the Archaic period defines the Māori's first arrival and initial adaption and survival in New Zealand, the Classic period was marked by the development of their culture, traditions, lifestyle, and relationships. Since their arrival, the Māori people had spread throughout the two islands, forming small settlements. But, by the 18th century, they had ventured further into New Zealand's interior and formed much more permanent settlements. These settlements in the Classic era were much more dependent on farming. After decades of experimentation, the Māori people had developed techniques that allowed them to cultivate the crops they had in the Polynesian islands, including yam, taro—and, of course, the sweet potato. While the Māori continued to depend on hunting and fishing, New Zealand plants also became a staple of their diet. Some of the local flora introduced includes karengo (a type of seaweed), huhu grubs (a type of beetle), pikopiko (fern shoots), and various seeds, fruit, berries, and fungi. During this period, the Māori developed a distinctive diet that took inspiration (but differed greatly) from their Polynesian heritage. They began developing distinctive dishes, such as toroi, which is made from fresh mussels with the juice of pūhā (also known as watercress or sow thistle). During the Classic period, the Māori also discovered new methods of conserving food, extending way past the typical drying, fermenting, or storing in cool pits underground. As settlements became much more permanent, the Māori were no longer nomadically chasing one prey after another. It became more convenient to catch a large quantity of meat or fish or gather a large number of seeds at once and keep them stored throughout the winters when food was scarcer. To ensure rats could not get to the food, the Māori developed pātakas, which were storehouses built on a pole above the ground. Pātakas resembled little houses, sometimes with rather intricate wood carvings, and most of them could be accessed from a trapdoor below.

Māori Arts

During the Classic period, the Māori people achieved extremely high levels of artistry. Artistry is certainly in the Māori genes, as the Polynesians were known to leave intricate statues and carvings around the world, the most iconic example being on Easter Island. But, isolated from their native lands, the Māori developed their own distinctive art forms.

Easter Island statues.
Ian Sewell, CC BY-SA 3.0 <http://creativecommons.org/licenses/by-sa/3.0/>, via Wikimedia Commons; https://commons.wikimedia.org/wiki/File:AhuTongariki.JPG

In general, Māori art is divided into four main categories: raranga (weaving), whakairo (carving), tā moko (tattooing), and peitatanga (painting). As with most older art forms, raranga came out of a place of necessity, as the Māori began weaving flax into fishing nets and ketes (baskets) for mainly utilitarian purposes. During the Classic period, as the Māori became more sedentary, the women were able to focus on using their raranga skills to create more intricate, symbolic pieces, such as dresses, skirts, and Korowai, which are traditional Māori cloaks. Every tribe's weaving looked different and included items integral to their community, such as natural dyes, feathers, and local plants.

While most of the descendants of the Polynesian explorers engage in some form of traditional tattooing or symbolic body scarring, the Māori developed their own distinctive markings known as tā moko. In the Classic period, tā moko tattoos were typically given to nobility or those of higher social rank. Today, elite rank is not required for Māoris to get tā moko tattoos, and it is much more common. Tā moko tattoos are split into two categories: Mataora for men and moko kauae for women. Both are typically on the face, but women's tā moko is usually on the lips and chin. Other than for social rank, Māori would get tā moko on other parts of their bodies to honor lost relatives. This mourning practice was especially common in women, who would cut themselves and add in pigment, shells, and other objects that represented their lost ones. The lines in the face ta moko tattoos are known as manawas (hearts), and they are drawn along the lines of the face in swirling patterns, representing the person's life's journey and the journey of their ancestors.

Portrait of a Young Māori Woman with Moko *(1891) by Louis John Steele.*
https://commons.wikimedia.org/wiki/File:Louis_John_Steele_-_Portrait_of_a_young_Maori_woman_with_moko_-_Google_Art_Project.jpg

Originally, before the Europeans brought needles to New Zealand, tā moko was applied using broad-toothed combs and chisel blades, known as uhi, that were dipped into naturally- obtained pigments and carved into the skin with the help of mallets called tās.

Tā moko tattoos are completely wrapped up in symbolism and therefore play a huge part in explaining the Māori's beliefs and traditions.

Māori Mythology and Beliefs

Although the Māori religion is now known as whakapono, this word was introduced by Europeans. The Māori people do not have a name for their belief system, but their spirituality is prevalent in every aspect of life, and at the base of their beliefs are the atua (gods). While entire books could be written about Māori atua and traditions, and each tribe has slightly different beliefs, many Māori gods hold both supernatural and natural powers. In most retellings of the creation of the world, there was total darkness in which a couple, Ranginui (sky father, also known as Rangi, or the heavens) and Papatūānuku (earth mother, also known as Papa) birthed children. These children wanted to experience light, so they tried to separate their parents, pushing the heavens (the sky) away from the earth—in other words, pushing Ranginui away from Papatūānuku. All Ranginui and Papatūānuku became atua of various natural elements, such as wind, forest, sea, and cultivated and uncultivated foods. The youngest of these children was Rūaumoko, the god of earthquakes and volcanoes, which were of course extremely prevalent during the Māori's early years in New Zealand. Before there was a word for these natural disasters, the Māori used the word Rūaumoko, as he embodied these events, and they were known as "the trembling current that scars the earth." It is assumed that the word moko (tattoo) originates from Rūaumoko. Other notable gods in the Māori religion were those of war, which would be especially relevant in the years after the Archaic period.

Māori Wars

Unlike the Archaic period, which was rather peaceful overall, the Classic Māori period was marked by tribal warfare remembered through orally-transmitted legends passed down for centuries. Until the arrival of the Europeans, nothing was written down, making it difficult to be sure about the exact details, dates, and effects of the battles, especially when details can be lost through generations of storytelling. For example, the story of one Māori legendary fight known as the battle of Pukekaikiore, which took place on North Island, describes how it was custom at the time for victors to eat the remaining defeated tribe and how the champions at the battle of Pukekaikiore crushed the other tribe so badly it was like a feast. Hāngī is a traditional Māori cooking technique that uses an umu (earth oven), which cooks food over heated rocks. The defeated were sent to the umu, and the hāngī feast was so large it was as if they were eating rats (which were everywhere), Therefore the battle was called the Pukekaikiore—"puke" meaning hill, "kai" meaning food, and "kiore" meaning a Polynesian rat. Regardless of the truth behind these claims, the mountain in the center of North Island, where the battle is said to have taken place, is still known as Pukekaikiore.

Although little is known for sure, it can be assumed that the Māori tribes fought about food, land, and social issues, which became more prevalent as the tribes diverged and developed their own beliefs and lifestyles during the Classic era. After the first contact with the Europeans, guns and firearms were introduced into New Zealand, completely changing tribal warfare. While battles were often described as bloody and deadly, they were likely on a much smaller scale and less horrendous than after the introduction of firearms. That said, the Māori tribes were obviously quite skilled in fighting by the time the Europeans arrived, and their first contact with the newcomers was violent and deadly for the Europeans.

Some evidence remains that helps us understand what battles may have been like before the arrival of the Europeans. Forts known as pā spread throughout New Zealand, mostly on the North Island. To avoid time-consuming building projects for these battles that usually did not last long, the Māori tribes used rivers, mountains, and swamps as natural barriers.

A pa built on a peninsular hilltop, using water and elevation as its natural barriers.
https://commons.wikimedia.org/wiki/File:Model_Of_Maori_Pa_On_Headland.jpg

A war dance known as the haka, used to intimidate and show off to enemies, was also passed down through generations of Māori. Unlike people from other territories, the Māoris rarely used projectile weapons such as bows and arrows or spears. Instead, most battles were fought hand-to-hand using various weapons or tools. According to legends, training for battle was an integral part of a young man's life. Many traditional Māori songs sung to the young or games played by children involved warfare somehow. For example, a game known as ti rakāu, where children would throw sticks to each other on beat to a song, was used to improve physical stamina, reflexes, and tolerance. The sticks used were quite large, especially in children's hands. This game, which appears more like an impressively-choreographed dance, is still practiced today.

People of all ages constantly trained, focusing on increasing their strength. This is apparent in the use of poi, which were essentially weighted balls at the end of strings. Today, poi are used for a dance of the same name. They are swung in patterns as the artist sings, dances, or both in beat. The poi used today are usually less traditional, and some have long strings or flags attached. The more notable poi dances involve poi on fire, which creates incredible illusions of fiery circles in the air.

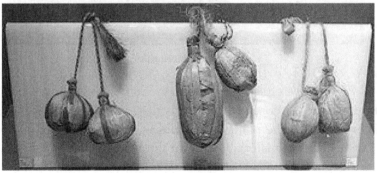

Early 20th-century poi.
Lianne Maitland, CC BY-SA 3.0 <https://creativecommons.org/licenses/by-sa/3.0>, via Wikimedia Commons; https://commons.wikimedia.org/wiki/File:SCMpoi.jpg

A performer using poi.
Stefan-Xp, CC BY-SA 3.0 <http://creativecommons.org/licenses/by-sa/3.0/>, via Wikimedia Commons; https://commons.wikimedia.org/wiki/File:Flammenjongleur.jpg

One of the most common weapons discovered from the Classic era of Māori warfare is the patu, an in-hand weapon similar to a club made from various natural materials. One of the main materials used to create patus was basalt, a volcanic rock solid enough to end someone's life if the weapon is used properly. Patus would also be made from whalebone, other rocks, or wood. Another weapon that was much more valued by Māori people—so much so that it was often passed down for generations—was the mere pounamu. It was usually made from jade and could target the head or ribs in close-contact fighting, similar to the patu.

Two of the more beautiful weapons that showed off the Māori's intricate wood carving skills were the wahaika (another paddle/club-like weapon) and the taiaha, which was more like a staff.

A wahaika.
https://commons.wikimedia.org/wiki/File:Maori_Zeremonialkeule_Museum_Rietberg_RPO_5.jpg

Māori Community and Homes

As the Māori spread throughout the New Zealand islands, smaller groups split off and settled, forming their own tribes known as iwis. Iwis greatly varied in size; the tribes could range from a few dozen to hundreds or thousands of people. Depending on the size of the population, the iwi might split up into hapūs (sub-tribes) and divided by whānau (family), class, or age. Iwis would build maraes, which were complexes that would include a wharenui, marae ātea, wharekai, as well as toilets and showers. Wharenui were beautiful wood-carved buildings used for everything from sleeping to meetings, religious practice, celebrations, funerals, school, training, and more. Wharenui can also be called whare tīpuna (ancestral houses), as the houses were usually named after an ancestor of the tribe or a legendary, mythological Māori.

A wharenui.
https://commons.wikimedia.org/wiki/File:Tanenuiarangi.jpg

The open, cleared-out yard in front of the wharenui was known as the marae ātea. Since this space was the embodiment of the atua (god) Tūmatauenga, who oversees war and human activities, this open lawn was typically used for meetings, discussions, and training when the weather was good. Maraes greatly differed from iwi to iwi, depending on the size of the group, their climate, and beliefs, which was usually apparent in their marae ātea. Some maraes were just a few structures, while others were more like an entire town, with large families having their own wharenui.

The last component of a marae was a wharekai, which was both a cooking area and a dining hall, usually large enough to hold a whole iwi. Visitors can only walk into a marae if they are formally welcomed, after which they would participate in a pōwhiri, a formal welcoming ceremony involving a speech (whaikōrero), singing, and food. This points to how sacred these spaces were to the tribes who lived there.

Māori Social Order

Unlike in other territories, social order in the Māori Classic era was more prevalent overall than family. While some importance was placed on one's immediate family later on (as land, items of worth, and title could be passed down within a family), the relationship between parents and children was not usually more significant than relationships with other people in an iwi. Typically, land was passed down to other members of the tribe rather than one's family. Raising children was a responsibility shared by the whole tribe, and adoption was common, serving a similar purpose to marriage—often to aid in political dealings. While there were separate classes within iwis, the labels were not as strict as in other societies. Each tribe was essentially split into three main social classes: the rangatira, the tauwareware, and the taurekareka.

In the Māori language, *rangatira* translates to "high rank, noble, chief, or leader." Within the rangatira, there were subsects. The general rangatira group typically included the elders of a tribe, known as the kaumātua, who often made up councils and advised leaders. The head chief of the tribe, known as the ariki, was also the highest of the rangatira class, and this was usually a title passed down through blood. Although most lineages were untracked, the most important rangatira's children would take the leadership role in the succession of his father. In some cases where male lineage was unknown, a child could be brought into the lineal order through his mother, either through blood or marriage. However, the ariki was always male, and descendance through male lineage was preferred. While there were many wars to claim power from arikis, the few who achieved chiefdom without lineage usually spent years rising in rank and proving their competence. These leaders who achieved chiefdom out of ritual status were known as rangatira paraparau, meaning "false leader." Although women could hold some important positions, especially elderly women, most iwis still restricted women from holding any real leadership positions. Usually, a woman could not even speak during a meeting.

The next class within Māori tribes was tauwareware, which essentially translates to "commoners." However, considering most settlements were started from very small groups, most people could claim some relation to one of the rangatira. Most people in an iwi were tauwareware and carried out their chief's commands. The tohunga was another subclass of note that could be within the rangatira or tauwareware. A tohunga was essentially a master of a skill or practice. Tohunga varied from religious experts to building or carving experts, healers, or navigators. Regardless, they were an elite class of their own within the iwi. Within the Māori belief system, there is a concept called tapu, which basically means something, someone, or someplace is sacred. Ariki were tapu because of their high status, as were tohunga. When a thing or person became tapu, there were strict rules about how it or they should be treated. Often, people who were tapu could not even touch food or be approached by others.

In this painting titled *Tohunga under Tapu*, by Gottfried Lindauer, a child is feeding a tohunga, who is an expert in dealing with the deceased. His sacred practice of handling the body parts of the dead made him tapu.
https://commons.wikimedia.org/wiki/File:Tohunga_under_Tapu.jpg

After the settlement of Europeans, tohunga would become controversial, as they became likened to using sorcery or black magic. The final group within the iwi was the taurekareka, which translates to "slave." While there were people of higher or lower ranks within the commoner class, it was most typical for slaves to be captives from other tribes taken in war. Although they were slaves who had few liberties, intermarriage was allowed and common with low-ranking tauwareware. The offspring of intermarriage was not bound to be a slave, making slavery a lot less binding than in other territories around the world.

Māori Marriage and Relationship Customs Pre-European Contact

European explorers who eventually made it to New Zealand often written about how different the Māori's views on marriage, relationships, and sexuality were from typical European standards. As in many countries around the world, it was not uncommon for the most important men—arikis, impressive soldiers, and other leaders in the community—to have multiple wives. Similar to other nations that practiced polyamory, married women could not have multiple partners and were expected to stay loyal to their husbands. However, where Māoris differed from these other nations is that pre-marriage (rather modern) dating and sexual relationships were not frowned upon. In a quote from Georg Forster, who was on one of James Cook's journeys to New Zealand, he says: "Their ideas of female chastity are, in this respect so different from ours, that a girl may favour a number of lovers without any detriment to her character; but if she marries, conjugal fidelity is exacted from her with the greatest rigour" (Forster, 1772). This liberal view on female virginity was not applied to the daughters of high-ranking rangatira, known as puhi, who were often married off for political arrangements, as with European monarchy. That said, arranged marriages were not only for Māori elites; most people in an iwi were married for various practical arrangements. Typically, the families or tribe leaders of the couple would meet and discuss how the arranged relationship could benefit both sides. Wiremu Maihi Te Rangikāheke, an iwi leader in the mid-19th century, is quoted as saying that, to win over a young woman's family, a young man's family gave them "two pieces of land, two dogskin cloaks, two greenstone ornaments, two canoes, two fine flax cloaks, six nets, four bird spears, three whalebone clubs, a maipi spear, a tewhatewha club, and one turuhi weapon. It is not as if a woman were a thing of small worth. Remember that food comes from the earth, sea-food from the net, and man from woman" (Rangikāheke, quoted by Bruce Biggs, 1970).

Māori People Pre-European Contact

As mentioned earlier, by the first contact with Europeans, an estimated 100,000 Māori were living in New Zealand. Since this number is estimated by Europeans, who only visited the coast of the islands, it is very possible that 200,000 or more people were living throughout New Zealand. It is believed that Māori people continued to use and construct canoes to travel back and forth within the Cook Straight between the North and South Island, most likely for trade. Most trade is believed to have been conducted among those living on the same island. Māori iwis on the coast would trade seafood, while tribes living inland would exchange all types of foods, wood, rocks, and minerals. Tribes that settled on smaller islands also had different resources worth trading, which kept them connected to those living on the main two islands. For example, those living on the volcanic Mayor Island (known as Tūhua) had obsidian, while those living on the North Island had basalt, and those living in the South Island had jade—all of which were important materials in Māori toolmaking and construction. Although the islands' natives all speak different dialects, and there are some branches, continued trading and contact maintained one main Māori language, known as te reo Māori. *Te Reo* literally translates to "language," so te reo Māori means the language of the Māori. Because of this, it is often referred to as simply the Māori language. Until the 19th century, te reo Māori had no written language, and stories were only conveyed orally or through various art forms, such as paintings, symbols, and carvings.

As illustrated in the last chapter, by the 19th century, the Māori people had built up a significantly rich and distinctive culture. Having arrived in their new lands much later than most first people, the Māori are unlike most indigenous peoples around the world. Despite being a breeding ground of natural disasters, by the 13th century, New Zealand had a stable environment, no real predators, and a wide variety of naturally-occurring food sources. The Māori were able to become sedentary within a few decades of their arrival in the new land, which gave them centuries to build villages, art forms, and agricultural techniques not possible for nomadic groups living in other territories. The Māori also did not have to deal with European contact until the 17th century, and Europeans did not settle in New Zealand until the 19th century. Unlike in most newly-claimed lands, the Māori population would outnumber the European population until the 1860s, nearly two centuries after the first European contact with New Zealand (covered in the next chapter), which makes for an interesting and convoluted history.

Chapter 3 – The Dutch Discovery of New Zealand, Mapmaking, and Its Naming (1600–1642)

The Creation of the Dutch East India Company

In the 16th and 17th centuries, the European powerhouse nations were all competing to claim lands outside of Europe that could provide precious minerals, new profitable resources, and a place to build new settlements. Although it is often overlooked during this time compared to England, France, and Spain, the Netherlands' economy grew rapidly as various trading companies were formed. These smaller companies had built up trading connections with European and Asian territories and had set up bases in Sri Lanka, India, and Indonesia. To compete with the other European powerhouses in the 17th century, these companies joined together in 1602 to create the notorious Dutch East India Company. As a united, powerful force focused solely on growing financially, the Dutch East Indian Company continued to send out explorers searching for new lands that could provide valuable resources or trade alliances.

The Dutch Discovery of Australia

Although there had always been rumors of land somewhere in the southern Pacific Ocean, Europeans were never truly sure until Dutch explorer Willem Janszoon of the Dutch East Indian Company was the first to spot Australia in 1606. He named this large continent "Nieu

Zeeland," after the Zeeland province in the Netherlands, although the name didn't stick. So, while Willem Janszoon did not discover New Zealand, he was the first European to discover the massive land masses in the southern Oceanic region. Until its discovery, Australia was rumored to be filled with valuable resources, such as gold and other precious minerals; however, Janszoon and his team were met not with profitable products but with hostile people. Despite having an unpleasant time in Australia, Willem Janszoon claimed the land previously known as Terra Australis Incognita ("unknown south land") for the Dutch. After Janszoon's discovery, many Dutch explorers sailed around Australia. But it would not be until four decades later that their adventures in the Southern Hemisphere would lead the Dutch to New Zealand.

The Dutch Discovery of New Zealand

After the discovery that confirmed the existence of land in the Southern Hemisphere, the Dutch East India Company had been planning to send another Dutchman to officially explore this territory and see what it had to offer. Since these lands were surrounded by hard-to-navigate waters, the company had to invest in an expedition and put its faith in a captain capable of reaching these nearly unreachable lands. Abel Janszoon Tasman had proven his worth for nearly a decade after exploring Indonesia, Japan, Taiwan, Cambodia, and other nations for the company; thus, he was chosen to lead the ambitious journey to the "Great South Land." Tasman finally reached a landmass in 1642, but it was not the Great South Land of Australia that had been originally named Nieu Zeeland. Instead, Tasman and his crew came across an island from which another large, high-lying land was spotted. While he knew this land was not Australia, Tasman thought he had miss-navigated and somehow ended up in South America, perhaps near the Le Maire Strait and Staten Landt, which had been discovered by another Dutch explorer named Jacob Le Maire. Staten Landt was believed to be a vague coastline extending from South America into the Southern Pacific region where Australia was supposed to be.

Why New Zealand was Named Staten Landt

Although it was disproved in the late 16th century, during the 1500s, Europeans believed that South America and the "unknown land in the Southern Hemisphere" (Terra Australia Incognita) were connected. When Le Maire spotted a vague landmass near South America, he named it Staten Landt, which was likely just a nearby island. Although cartographers knew it was not connected to Australia after many explorers had sailed around the two land masses, Europeans were not sure exactly how far Australia was from South America. This would mean that Staten Landt was likely somewhere between the two continents. Thus, when Tasman spotted New Zealand, knowing it was not Australia, he assumed he must have veered off course in the Southern Hemisphere's choppy waters and ended up in Staten Landt. So, he officially declared New Zealand's Southern Island Staten Landt in 1642. Of course, Tasman had not veered as far off course as he thought. Although New Zealand is technically between Australia and South America, it is much closer to the former. It is now known that Le Maire's Staten Landt (known as Isla de los Estados) is actually an island just a few dozen kilometers off the coast of Argentina, while Tasman's Staten Landt was New Zealand, some ten thousand kilometers away from its namesake.

In Tasman's 1642-1643 expedition, he would completely miss Australia and travel along the western coast of New Zealand's two islands and the southern coast of Tasmania.

After other Dutch explorers made their way to South America and Le Maire's Staten Landt, Tasman revisited the Southern Hemisphere and finally explored Australia's coastline. This map of Australia, New Zealand, and Tasmania was drawn up officially sometime after Tasman's journey. Cartographers were still very unsure of how the territories looked. However, it was now understood that New Zealand was separate from Le Maire's South American Staten Landt and that New Zealand was close to Australia.

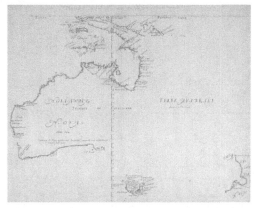

What early explorers thought the region looked like.
https://commons.wikimedia.org/wiki/File:Thevenot_-_Hollandia_Nova_detecta_1644.png

New Zealand's Names Origination

Once it was understood that New Zealand's Staten Landt islands were different from Le Maire's Staten Landt, a Dutch cartographer who worked for the Dutch East India Company, renamed the land Nieuw Zeeland. The new name was inspired by the Dutch province of Zeeland, which literally translates as "Sealand," named appropriately because it is made up of numerous islands and peninsulas, not so different from New Zealand. Although this was, of course, the name that would stick around, it must be noted that by this time, New Zealand had already been given another name by the Māori living there. The North Island was known as Aotearoa, and the South Island was known as Te Wahipounamu; together, New Zealand was Aotearoa me Te Wahipounamu, meaning "North Island and South Island." According to Māori translations, Aotearoa means "long white cloud," referring to the fact that the North Island was so mountainous it was surrounded by cloud formations that made it easy to identify by the Māori. Te Wahipounamu is said to translate to "land of greenstone," named for its abundance of jade. Since there were so many individual iwis, there were many names for New Zealand's islands. However, these are the main two still used by the Māori today.

Chapter 4 – First European Contact with the Māori and Tasman's Journeys (1642–1769)

Tasman and His Crew's Adventures in Tasmania

In August 1642, Tasman and his crew began sailing south from Batavia, Indonesia. After a delayed supply restock in Mauritius, the expedition finally reached land in the Southern Hemisphere in November. While they had been aiming for Australia, choppy waters, poor visibility and strong westerly winds resulted in an overcorrection in navigation, landing the Tasman and his crew south of their goal, in Tasmania (then Van Diemen's Land). The group finally debarked at the start of December. Along the coast of Tasmania, they discovered lots of lumber and vegetables. The crew collected water in a nearby stream and picked some vegetables they assumed had grown naturally until their explorations led them to signs that perhaps the vegetables were not "growing by the will of God." Although Tasman himself remained on the ship, his crew discovered extremely tall trees with wedges cut out of them, indicating that perhaps humans had created notches to climb up to catch birds or other prey. The group also heard sounds they assumed were human, leading Tasman to write: "So there can be no doubt there must be men here of extraordinary stature" (Tasman, 1642). Although neither Tasman nor his crew encountered any people in Tasmania, their short exploration effectively proved human existence on the island and confirmed that Tasmania was a separate island from Australia and New Zealand.

Tasman's Expedition to New Zealand

After quickly realizing they had obviously veered off course and spending some time exploring this newly-discovered land, Tasman and his crew embarked on their ship to continue sailing east. By mid-December, the crew found themselves still not in Australia but near the mid-western coast of the Southern Island of New Zealand (then Staten Landt), somewhere between Hokitika and Okarito. The ship hugged the Southern Island's western coastline and continued north to Cape Farewell. They docked near Cape Farewell on December 17, and the following morning, the crew wrote that they saw smoke rising from the shore, proving the existence of humans on the island. That day, they continued sailing around the northern edge of the Southern Island until finally docking again that evening in the very shallow waters near Taupo Point. On this day, it became obvious to Tasman that New Zealand had two islands, as the travelogue described another higher-lying coastline nearby.

The Europeans' First Interaction with the Māori

As the previous evening in Cape Farewell had indicated, humans were living on the southern New Zealand island. A few men from the ship debarked while docked near Taupō Point, searching for water, but they did not run into anybody during this short exploration. In the evening, after all the crew members had returned to the ship, Tasman and his crew again spotted human activity along the coast, this time in the form of light from fires. Historians now believe that the fires and smoke spotted by the Europeans may have actually been a series of signals sent by the Māori tribes, specifically the Ngāti Tūmatakōkiri iwi, warning people up the coast of the unfamiliar ships nearby.

According to Tasman, once his men "had returned on board, the people in the two prows [boats] began to call to us, and that with a coarse, rough voice, but we could not understand in the least what they said" (Tasman, 1642). As this quote indicates, it seemed that members of the Māori tribes, who had been watching the Dutch from land, had come out on what seemed to be two boats and begun trying to make contact with the newcomers. According to Tasman, the Māori also used some sort of trumpet to warn their tribes, make their presence known to the Europeans, or perhaps ward off the newcomers. Either way, the crew of the two ships Tasman had been commanding, the *Heemskerck* and *Zeehaen*, responded with their own trumpets. After hours of this interaction that accounts for the first contact between Europeans and Māori, the Māori boats returned to shore. Although the interaction had seemed friendly enough, Tasman spent the night preparing his crew for potential conflict.

Overnight, the ships had been outfitted for war. The following morning, feeling safer, Tasman tried a different approach. He displayed various linens, weapons, and other sought-after items, hoping to coax the Māori to make the first move and come closer. However, the boats that had once again appeared returned to shore again without interaction on this second day. After this, Tasman and his officials met and decided it would be best to get closer to the shoreline, without actually going ashore, to make an assertive but friendly gesture. According to Tasman's notes, he and his crew believed the Māori people would want to be peaceful, following the interactions of the previous days.

Tasman sent a few men out in a small boat to get closer to shore, where they were met by one Māori canoe, known as a waka, that had been waiting for them. Before long, seven more wakas joined. Seeing that his crew was overwhelmed, Tasman called his men back. Whether it was the Māori's plan all along or they saw this communication as a threat, those aboard one of the wakas invaded the small Dutch boat following Tasman's orders, resulting in a violent skirmish. Since the Europeans were not expecting an attack, this battle resulted in the death of four of Tasman's men. Tasman's crew quickly fired off a canon at the Māori people, but they had returned to their waka in time; they avoided the fire and returned to shore unscathed. After this violent interaction, Tasman named the bay where the Dutch boats had been docked (now known Golden Bay) Moordenaers Baij, which literally translates to "Murderers' Bay." Over a dozen Māori wakas began coming at the Dutch boats, but once his remaining men rejoined the ship, Tasman ordered his crew to pull up the anchors and sail northeast away from their attackers.

The end of December of 1642 brought bad weather. Thus, the Dutch ships could not continue traveling north. Instead, they sailed a short distance east to D'Urville Island. The weather remained poor until the day after Christmas, so the Dutchmen celebrated Christmas on their ships with wine and meat from pigs aboard.

Why the Māori's First Interactions with Europeans Were So Negative

Historians have theorized various reasons that might explain the Māori people's sudden attack on the Dutch in their first interaction. One is that the Ngāti Tūmatakōkiri tribe, the first iwi to make contact with the Europeans, had been involved in many skirmishes over land in the past century; this may explain their lack of trust in the newcomers. The Ngāti Tūmatakōkiri had initially lived on North Island, but in the mid-16th century, they relocated to the northern tip of South Island, which led to many battles with iwis already living there. Over the latter half of the 16th century, the Ngāti Tūmatakōkiri established their power in the region; however, they continued to be under attack throughout the 17th century. In fact, these land battles between the Ngāti Tūmatakōkiri and other tribes would continue well into the 19th century. The Ngāti Tūmatakōkiri iwi may have simply been trying to protect their land, their families, and perhaps their crops—specifically, the kūmara (sweet potato), which was in its peak production season—from what seemed to be a threat.

Another explanation for why the Māori were so defensive toward the Dutch is their spirituality. In Māori folklore, there is a supernatural being known as a patupaiarehe: a pale Caucasian with blonde or light hair, no tattoos, and the appearance of a normal human. Despite looking like normal light-skinned Europeans, patupaiarehes were aggressive and said to steal women and children from tribes, specifically those who stole the patupaiarehes' land. The Dutch, who appeared almost exactly like the oral descriptions of the patupaiarehe, may have alarmed the already-cautious Māori. According to Tasman's descriptions, large groups of people were on the shoreline, which may also indicate an important meeting, ceremony, or funeral. If it was a meeting, it might indicate that the group was preparing for a battle; if it was a funeral, the Māori, who hold death in very high regard, may have been extremely superstitious.

The last reason historians believe the Māori tribe may have suddenly attacked the Dutch is that perhaps news of Europeans arriving in other territories had reached New Zealand. Although we have no concrete proof that settlers of different Pacific islands visited each other, it is known that the Polynesian settlers were able navigators. As the Māori people continued to sail, it is possible that another more southern tribe, or even a tribe from another territory such as Tasmania, may have warned the Māori people about European-looking people (which could even explain the physical description of the patupaiarehe in Māori mythology).

Of course, it could have been much simpler than all of this. The Europeans' actions may have seemed much more aggressive than intended. Perhaps Tasman's idea of displaying weapons and other sought-after items was taken as a threat, as could have been the trumpet responses and moving closer to shore.

The Rest of Tasman's Journey After Meeting the Māori

While anchored just off the coast of D'Urville Island, the crew could tell there was a strong current, indicating a passage between the North and South Islands. However, when the crew pulled up their anchor again on December 26, they could not enter the passage due to strong winds. This passage is now known as Cook's Strait—but it may have had another name if the weather had been different or if Tasman had decided to include his theory in his notes. The ships continued north, hugging the western coast of the North Island but never debarking. Around January 4, 1643, the ships reached the northernmost point of New Zealand's North Island, which Tasman named Cape Maria van Diemen after the wife of Governor General Anthony van Diemen. Despite having supplies for twelve months, the crew had expected to be able to debark and get fresh water along the voyage. But, during the tumultuous five months, not once did Tasman's crew make it to shore. In other words, although they helped map out New Zealand and had the first interactions with the Māori, Tasman and his crew never set foot in New Zealand. The crew finally went ashore on a small group of islands that Tasman named the Three Kings Islands. These islands did provide the fresh water the crew had been looking for without any conflict, as the Three Kings Islands were uninhabited, just as they are today. Despite the islands' lack of settlements, Tasman spotted a few dozen people, who did not notice the crew. He noted agricultural fields, indicating that the Māori people had been using wakas to travel to these lands to grow crops.

Tasman continued along the Pacific Islands and followed the coast of New Guinea until finishing his journey in Batavia (now Jakarta, Indonesia), the capital of the Dutch East Indies at the time. Although Tasman's journey helped map out the coastline of New Zealand and served as a rough first introduction between European people and the

Māori, the Dutch East India Company was not pleased with his expedition. This was made clear by the Dutch Batavia Council even before Tasman's return to the Netherlands. The council was quoted as saying: "What there is in this Southland, whether above or under the earth, continues unknown, since the men have done nothing beyond sailing along the coast; he who makes it his business to find out what the land produces must walk all over it, which these discoverers pretend to have been out of their power" (Batavia Council, 1644). Tasman failed in his mission to find and explore Australia and also failed to find any profitable resources during his detours in New Zealand.

Why New Zealand Was Not Visited Again After Tasman

Despite his failures in exploring Terra Australis, Governor General van Diemen and the Dutch East Indian Company decided to send Tasman out to lead yet another expedition, this time to find a route from Batavia to Chile. Unlike lands discovered in the Southern Hemisphere during Tasman's last journey, Chile had proven profitable for the Netherlands when gold was discovered. Tasman departed on his journey in 1644, accompanied by Dutch navigator, explorer, and cartographer Frans Jacobszoon Visscher, who had also been an important leader in Tasman's 1642 journey. However, ironically, when Tasman tried to reach South America this time, he finally made it to Australia. Tasman and his crew on the three ships he commanded explored Australia's northern coastline before returning to Batavia, having failed his original mission. Although Tasman's journal of the journey has been lost, van Diemen is paraphrased as saying, "Tasman had found nothing profitable, only naked beach-runners without rice" (Van Diemen, 2010). Tasman's expedition helped map out the Southern Hemisphere and gave us insight into the Māori and indigenous people living throughout Oceania at the time. However, despite how Tasman's journeys helped historians and cartographers, they were seen as a failure. Land in Terra Australis was deemed unprofitable and a waste of time and money to re-explore. Thus, the Dutch focused on trade in the East Indies. Australia, New Zealand, and Tasmania were mostly ignored by Europeans for another century. While there were further visits to Australia in the decades after Tasman's journeys, these were mostly by accident. Although the Dutch were the first to discover New Zealand, contact its people, and map out the land, they would have little more to do with the islands. It is estimated that there were only about 130 Dutch in New Zealand before World War II.

The Māori after Tasman

Although there is little mention of the Dutch encounter in Māori oral history, we can assume that news of these threatening fair-skinned travelers spread throughout New Zealand. While it is hard to track down the exact origination date of Māori legends, and the mythology surrounding Patupaiarehe certainly existed pre-European contact, we can assume that more details were added to the lore after the Dutch interaction. As mentioned earlier, Patupaiarehe were fair-skinned, light-haired, European-looking supernatural fairies who stole wives and children from Māori men and were disgusted with Māori habits, art, lifestyle, religion, and cooking. The patupaiarehe would not paint their face with kōkōwai (red ochre pigment used for dying carved wood and face painting, specifically for war) and looked down on karakias, which are Māori spiritual prayers. While Tasman's journals indicate that the Māori had little interaction with the Dutch, patupaiarehe mythology was certainly prevalent by the early 18th century.

One reason the patupaiarehe legends may closely resemble stereotypical Europeans, who would not arrive in New Zealand for over 100 years, is that some historians believe Māori people actually traveled to Europe after Tasman visited New Zealand. New Zealand historian Vincent O'Malley has dedicated his life to the belief that exploration was not only done by European superpowers. According to an interview with O'Malley conducted by Radio New Zealand's show, Nine to Noon, he believes that "By 1840, Māori had traveled to every continent on the Earth, including Antarctica" (O'Malley, 2015). While many of these travels were conducted with European navigators, it has been proven that the Māori and their Polynesian ancestors were capable of incredible feats of sailing and navigation. Therefore, Māori may have traveled to other territories, most likely those that Europeans had visited or colonized. But it is possible they reached Europe itself.

Other than their relationship with the Europeans, the Māori continued to develop, strengthen, and improve their traditions, habits, and lifestyle from the Classic period. They had extensive fields of bottle gourds, sweet potatoes, and yams, which the Māori established to feed their ever-growing communities.

Chapter 5 – James Cook and the British Claim to New Zealand (1769–1780)

James Cook and The Royal Society

While the Māori enjoyed development uninterrupted by European contact post-Tasman's journey to New Zealand, a young Brit named James Cook was making his way up the ranks as a seaman. After years of apprenticing on ships and rising from mate to commander, Cook joined the Royal Navy and proved his abilities as a seaman and navigator.

Meanwhile, the Royal Society of London for Improving Natural Knowledge (often shortened to the Royal Society), a group of academics and intellectuals focused on discussing and discovering scientific and philosophical matters, was planning a journey to the Pacific Islands. Although much was still unknown about the islands, the Royal Society was not organizing an expedition to explore the territories. Instead, it was to observe astronomical phenomena. Between 1761 and 1769, the Royal Society had mapped out various locations where the transits of Venus could be observed. According to astronomers, Venus' travels would be visible from the South Pacific on June 3, 1769. Tracking this transit would allow the Royal Society to determine astronomical distances, such as between the Earth and the sun.

While many navigators had been considered for the expeditions, the Royal Society issued James Cook (having spent over two decades at sea) a membership to their elite group, knighting him with this quote: "[James Cook is] a gentleman skillful in astronomy, & the successful conductor of two important voyages for the discovery of unknown countries, by which geography & natural history have been greatly advantaged and improved, being desirous of the honour of becoming a member of this Society, we whose names are underwritten, do, from our personal knowledge testify, that we believe him deserving of such honour, and that he will become a worthy & useful member" (The Royal Society, 1776).

Unlike previous explorers, who were masters of navigation instructed to discover new claimable lands and find profitable resources abroad, James Cook was instructed to simply be a captain, navigating the ship so that the masters aboard could make discoveries and reach their destination. After much debate, it was decided that Tahiti would be the best place to observe the astronomical phenomenon. In August 1768, Cook left England aboard his ship, the *Endeavour*, alongside various members of the Royal Society, including astronomers, artists, and scientists. Two of the more notable members of the Royal Society aboard included the only twenty-six-year-old English botanist Joseph Banks and his Swedish botany assistant Daniel Solander.

The First Leg of the Journey in Tahiti

Although the Royal Society's name may imply nobility and riches, the group was mostly made up of scholarly intellectuals. Funding a trip around the world was not cheap, as it was necessary to pay for not only a ship, supplies, equipment (both for navigating and scientific purposes), and food but also the salaries of the seamen. To make the journey happen, the Royal Society was aided by the British Admiralty, which, according to members aboard the ship, gave Cook instructions sealed up in an envelope, only to be opened after the June 3rd astronomical phenomenon had been seen.

Unlike Tasman, James Cook did not reach New Zealand by accidental navigation. Starting in Brazil, Cook managed to reach Tahiti by way of Cape Horn, Chile, without much struggle in April 1769, nine months after leaving England. Of course, since the astronomical phenomenon was not scheduled to occur until June, Cook and the other Royal Society scientists spent nearly four months in Tahiti. While the astronomers set up makeshift observatories, the artists illustrated the island, Joseph Banks and Daniel Solander logged plant and animal species, and Cook explored Tahiti and the nearby islands.

Although Tahiti was claimed by the French in 1768 and would end up as an island in the French Polynesians, this astronomical event was globally recognized as so incredibly significant that it circumvented any land ownership. The French government not only allowed Cook and The Royal Society scientists to station in Tahiti to observe the natural phenomenon but also issued instructions to let Cook's ships sail freely. This is significant because 1768 was not long after the intensive Seven Years' War of 1756-1763. The war was catastrophic in Europe and caused France to lose land in North America to England, including all of Canada.

While in Tahiti, Cook and the other travelers tried to study the language of the indigenous Polynesians, learn their customs, and communicate with the local population. Unlike Tasman's experience in New Zealand, during the four months the Englishmen spent in Tahiti, they had some positive interactions with the Polynesians. One example of this is Joseph Banks and James Cook's relationship with Tupaia. According to travelogues, Tupaia was a Tahitian Polynesian priest who approached Cook, offering to help him navigate through the Pacific Islands and communicate with the local populations. In some accounts, Tupaia approached Banks, not Cook, and it was Banks who convinced Cook to allow Tupaia to join the expedition. Although all the Polynesian islands had developed distinctive languages (such as in New Zealand), their shared Polynesian heritage made it possible for Tupaia to communicate with them after hundreds of years of isolation.

While Tupaia himself had not done much exploring, he told Banks and Cook that his ancestors, specifically his father and grandfather, had been avid sailors. Together, they created a vague map of the Polynesian islands, both from Tupaia's descriptions and short trips from Tahiti.

Although Tupaia would prove indispensable on Cook's first expedition in the Pacific, the Europeans aboard were not all so comfortable with taking advice from an indigenous person. According to the 1987 book *Tupaia: The Remarkable Story of Captain Cook's Polynesian Navigator* by Joan Druett, a sailor aboard named Joseph Marra said: "[Tupaia] was a man of real genius, a priest of the first order, and an excellent artist: he was, however, by no means beloved by the *Endeavour*'s crew, being looked upon as proud and austere, extorting homage, which the sailors who thought themselves degraded by bending to an Indian, were very unwilling to pay, and preferring complaints against them on the most trivial occasions."

As planned, the passage of Venus in front of the sun was observed through blurry telescopes on June 3, 1769, but it would unfortunately turn out to be essentially pointless. Despite the astronomical discoveries being a disappointment, Cook's first journey would reveal many more important discoveries. After viewing the astronomical phenomena, Cook opened the written orders from the British Admiralty, which instructed him to continue sailing from Tahiti to claim and explore Terra Australis, specifically New Holland (Australia), which was believed to be rich in gold. According to journals of the time, the instructions ordered Cook to not only explore and map out Terra Australis but also "to observe the genius, temper, disposition and number of the natives, if there be any, and endeavor by all proper means to cultivate a friendship and alliance with them...You are also with the consent of the natives to take possession of convenient situations in the country, in the name of the King of Great Britain" (Hawke, Brett, Spencer, 1768).

Cook's Journey to New Zealand

Along with The Royal Society scientists and artists, Cook sailed with Tupaia, who would help him throughout the rest of his journey. The group left aboard the HMS *Endeavor* in late July or early August 1769, nearly a year after leaving England. Initially, Cook followed the navigation instructions given to him by the British Admiralty, which ordered him to sail south below latitude 40° S. However, Cook failed to find any land. This is likely because Tasman and other explorers had sailed from the southeast to reach the Pacific Islands, while Cook left from the northeastern island of Tahiti. Combining Tupaia's understanding of the region with Cook's navigation skills, the group reached New Zealand at the beginning of October 1769.

Arrival in New Zealand

According to legends, Cook had grown frustrated that he had not yet spotted New Zealand. Thus, he promised to reward whoever could spot land first with a prize of rum. It is also said that Cook promised he would name the land after whoever spotted it. On October 6, 1769, Nicholas Young, the assistant to a surgeon on board, spotted the eastern coastline of New Zealand's North Island. While it is unknown whether Nicholas received his fabled compensation of rum for spotting New Zealand, Cook did name the tip of the land Young Nick's Head.

Young Nick's Head is located in Poverty Bay, known as Tūranganui-a-Kiwa by the Māori population. Despite the legend that Cook would name the first land sighted after whoever spotted it, some historians believe that Young Nick's Head might not have been the first piece of New Zealand seen by Cook's men. While Young Nick's Head is certainly on the eastern coast of North Island, it is rather strange that it is so centrally located on New Zealand's North Island, as it is more likely that Cook would have spotted a more northern landmark first. Regardless of what was spotted first, Cook would anchor in Poverty Bay just near Young Nick's Head and, a few days later, take the first known European steps on New Zealand just near Tūranganui River.

Interestingly, the Māori who arrived in New Zealand some 400 years earlier also departed from the Polynesian islands. While it is not exactly certain which island they originated from or where they would have debarked, many historians assume the Māori people have roots in Tahiti. This means that Cook and his crew would have made a very similar journey to that of the Polynesian immigrants who became the Māori.

European Interactions with the Māori People

There are many different accounts of what the first days ashore were like. Some versions of Cook's first contact with the Māori people are peaceful and involve Tupaia making the first introductions. In one account, Tupaia tells Cook to sit on the sand and wait while he makes a speech explaining that he came in peace to the local people who intercepted them on the beach. Despite the language differences, Tupaia is described as communicating effortlessly with the local Māori people. Later, while in Australia, Cook is quoted as writing: "By means of Tupaia ... you would always get people to direct you from Island to Island and would be sure of meeting with a friendly reception and refreshments at every Island you came to" (Cook, 1770, quoted by Anne Salmond, 2016). In other accounts of Cook's first meeting with the Māori people, Tupaia is uninvolved, and the first interactions are not as peaceful. According to another account at the time, Cook and Banks (and maybe a few other men) go on land a few days after anchoring in Poverty Bay and surprise the unsuspecting Māori ashore, leading to a violent interaction and resulting in the death of at least one Māori man.

There are many reasons why these accounts of such an important meeting are so different. As mentioned in the quote by Joseph Marra, many of the sailors felt ashamed to be dependent on an indigenous man, so they may have left out his helpful communication in their accounts of the interaction. Also, during this year, Cook and his people traveled from island to island, meeting many different populations; even in New Zealand, the crew constantly encountered new Māori iwis. With all these "first interactions" with different Māori iwis and Polynesian tribes, accounts of the actual first interaction may have become jumbled. Future interactions between Māori and Europeans are described as mostly positive.

Whether the first interactions started as violent or peaceful, botanists Joseph Banks and Daniel Solander began logging flora and fauna in New Zealand within the next few days, and the crew began trading with the Māori people.

In this drawing by Tupaia from 1769, now held in the British Library, a Māori man exchanges a crayfish for a piece of cloth with a European man (apparently Joseph Banks).
https://commons.wikimedia.org/wiki/File:A_Maori_man_and_Joseph_Banks_exchanging_a_cray fish_for_a_piece_of_cloth,_c._1769.jpg

Cook's Impact on the Māori

Overall, when it comes to European accounts of the indigenous, it is difficult to tell the difference between exaggeration, truth, and lies. During 1769 and 1777, Cook visited New Zealand on three iconic Pacific expeditions, which allowed him to compare how the people and land had changed after European interaction. While it can be difficult to ascertain the impacts of Cook's (and other European) visits, Cook's accounts do provide some insight into life in New Zealand pre-settlement.

One example of the impact of Cook's voyages on the Māori people is the introduction of metal. Today, New Zealand's closest neighbor, Australia, is the world's top iron producer. However, the Māori never came into contact with iron until the British brought it over during Cook's first journey. Although the Māori were very modernized with carving, building, and tools, they were still living in somewhat of an advanced stone age as far as materials went. For example, to cut anything, they used shells or sharpened stones. According to Cook's later writings, crewmembers gave the Māori iron tools and showed them how they could be used to cut things more efficiently. Unlike stone or shells, metal could be sharpened to create a finer cut and reused for longer without wearing down. The British aboard the HMS *Endeavor* noted that pre-European arrival, the Māori had been using quite similar tools, just made with different materials, such as stone. On Cook's second journey to New Zealand in 1773, he brought iron hatchets; by the third journey in 1777, he noted metal seemed to be controlling the Māori people. Of course, this may be an exaggeration. But according to Cook's notes from his third voyage, metal hatchets were not used as much for cutting trees as for killing. Māori men were stealing or offering their daughters and wives to Europeans in exchange for metal tools.

Another notable impact of Cook's journeys was the introduction of new animals into the islands. While the botanists aboard spent their time studying the local flora and fauna, they were completely changing the species living on the lands they explored. As with most long-term expeditions, Cook's ships always had animals aboard, usually for feeding the crew and presenting as peace offerings to the indigenous populations. As explained in earlier chapters, chickens did not appear in New Zealand until the arrival of Europeans. On one of Cook's journeys, chickens were likely first introduced into New Zealand. The same could be said of many European crops. On every expedition, botanists would plant seeds or hand them out to the Māori to plant to study how they survived and evolved the next time they came back. One example of this is the release of goats in the Queen Charlotte Sound, specifically on Allports Island, which became known as Goat Island due to the overrunning of goats released by European travelers. While releasing new flora and fauna was not disastrous in New Zealand, it certainly impacted the lifestyle, diets, and habits of the Māori, who previously had no land mammals other than rats and dogs.

Although Cook certainly impacted the Māori, he mostly wrote of them with respect. He considered them more civilized and modern than the indigenous populations he had encountered in Tahiti and noted that they were much more sedentary than those living in Australia. While it is unknown exactly how much he interacted with the Māori, Tupaia's presence certainly helped Cook have a more positive experience than other Europeans, such as Tasman. On his first journey, Cook wrote: "[The Māori] are a strong, well made, active people as any we have seen yet, and all of them paint their bod[ie]s with red oker and oil from head to foot, a thing we have not seen before. Their canoes are large, well built and ornamented with carved work" (Cook, quoted by Lorraine Boissoneault, 2018).

Of course, Cook, alongside most European explorers of the time, is a controversial figure. While he was a hero to the British, he claimed the lands of the indigenous populations for England without their consent. Today, Cook is often viewed as a colonizer. While he certainly sped up England's colonization of New Zealand and other lands, many people (and historians) still defend Cook. Many claim he was simply a visitor, cartographer, scientist, and explorer who helped England better understand the Pacific Islands. How the British Crown proceeded with Cook's information is their fault. Historian and professor Glyndwr Williams argues that defending that Cook was "simply doing his job and had no colonization intentions" is not accurate either. According to Williams, "It would be as wrong to regard Cook as an unwitting agent of British imperialism as [it would be] to fall into the trap of judging him according to how we judge what happened afterwards. His command of successive voyages indicated both his professional commitment, and his patriotic belief that if a European nation should dominate the waters and lands of the Pacific, then it must be Britain" (Williams, 2004, quoted by Lorraine Boissoneault, 2018).

The negativity of Cook's journey toward New Zealand can be debated. Cook's journey brought weapons, such as hatchets, that could cause violence and diseases that likely killed millions of indigenous Polynesian people. Following his visits to other islands, native populations dropped by hundreds of thousands. The first stop of his journey, Tahiti, proves the perfect example. Cook estimated the population to be about 200,000 in 1769, but by the time the French began colonizing a century later, the population had dropped to about 7,000. Ultimately, Tupaia himself would die of a European disease, likely dysentery or malaria, while upon the HMS *Endeavor*.

A quote from Lorraine Boissoneault, a history writer for the *Smithsonian*, summarizes perfectly the modern view of Cook's journeys: "an empire-building project dressed with the trappings of science" (Boissoneault, 2018).

How Cook Helped England Understand New Zealand

Overall, Cook's journeys to New Zealand, which officially claimed the land for England, would completely change the islands forever and completely shift the British understanding of the Pacific Islands' landscape, people, and species. Alongside the scientists, artists, and botanists aboard, Cook and the other sailors kept detailed travelogues summarizing the people they met, how they dressed, the words they used, their lifestyle, customs, and their territory. Although Tasman had helped to dispel this belief, Cook's detailed mapmaking of the lands he explored proved that there was no Terra Australis, or at least not the way some Europeans had believed. While there was indeed "land down under," during the 17th century it was a common belief that Terra Australis would be a massive continent comparable to Asia and Europe, as the Earth had somewhat symmetrically balanced landmasses in both hemispheres. While Australia is huge, and New Zealand alone is 10 percent larger in landmass than the United Kingdom, these Pacific lands are nowhere near comparable to the Euro-Asian continent.

During his journeys, Cook kept a surprisingly accurate map of the coastlines he circumvented, which he used to map out the islands he visited. The only real differences between Cook's map and the maps we have today are that "Banks Island" (on the South Island's eastern coast) is not an island but a peninsula, and Cape South (at the southern tip of the Southern Island) is not a peninsula but an island (now known as Stewart Island).

The Rest of Cook's First Journey

Cook and his crew of scientists did not end their journey in New Zealand. They made their way around the entire world. After spending six months charting New Zealand and communicating with the Māori, Cook continued to Australia and Batavia (where Tupaia is said to have died of European disease), returning home to England by heading north after rounding the southwestern coast of Africa.

During his first journey, Cook also charted the eastern coast of Australia, claiming it for England. While in Australia, he encountered various indigenous tribes, of which he said: "The natives appear to be the most wretched people upon Earth. But in reality, they are far more happier than we Europeans being wholly unacquainted not only with the superfluous, but the necessary conveniences so much sought after in Europe. They are happy in not knowing the use of them. They live in tranquility, which is not disturbed by the inequality of condition. They set no value upon anything we gave them, and nor would they ever part with anything of their own" (Cook, 1824). While Australia's indigenous are extremely different from New Zealand's Māori, this quote demonstrates Cook's (and the general European) view of native people at the time. Of course, despite believing the native people were happy—happier than Europeans—Cook still strongly recommended that England colonize Australia, without mentioning much concern for the indigenous tribes he wrote about.

Cook's Subsequent Journeys

Since Tupaia died during the first Pacific journey, Cook's subsequent visits to New Zealand did not include his Tahitian guide. According to notes, when Cook landed in New Zealand in 1773 during his second voyage, the Māori tribes asked about Tupaia. Some accounts even describe the Māori people excitedly yelling Tupaia's name when they saw the British ships return to shore. Regardless, Tupaia's influence seemed to remain even without his presence. Cook and the other Europeans aboard his subsequent voyages seemed to maintain positive relations with the Māori tribes they encountered. While Cook would explore different areas of New Zealand during all his voyages, he managed to anchor in Ship Cove, located at the northern tip of South Island in the region of Queen Charlotte Sound. This location proved to be the perfect base, facilitating travel between both islands. The water near Ship Cove, which separates New Zealand's North and South Islands, was named Cook's Straight.

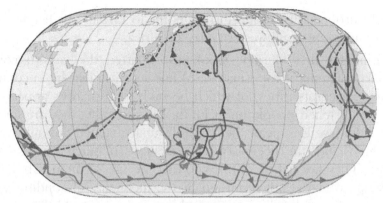

This map displays not only Cook's first journey (1768-1771) in red but also his second journey (1772-1775) in green and his third journey (1776-1779) in blue, of which stopped in New Zealand.

Jon Platek. Blank map by en:User:Reisio., CC BY-SA 3.0 <https://creativecommons.org/licenses/by-sa/3.0>, via Wikimedia Commons; https://commons.wikimedia.org/wiki/File:Cook_Three_Voyages_59.png

Before Cook died in Hawaii on his third Pacific journey in 1779, his and Banks' journal entries were published as *A Voyage Towards the South Pole and Round the World* (1777). While this book covered nearly all the lands Cook visited, he mentioned that New Zealand would be an ideal country to colonize and settle in and emphasized the intelligence of the Māori people.

Chapter 6 – French Explorers' Contacts with New Zealand Before Settlement and the Musket Wars (1770–1830)

Other Europeans in New Zealand

Although Cook and those aboard his voyages certainly had the largest impact on New Zealand, both for the Māori they encountered and the future of the islands, the British were not the only ones to visit New Zealand during the 18th century. After Tasman spotted New Zealand, European nations became aware of the new discovery in the Southern Hemisphere. However, it would not be until after Cook's voyages that the existence of New Zealand would become public knowledge. This certainly has a lot to do with the fact that Tasman advised against settling in New Zealand, while Cook—who had become somewhat of a celebrity after his voyages helped create the modern map of Earth—strongly promoted the colonization of the islands and spoke of the Māori's capabilities.

Marc-Joseph Marion du Fresne

While many different explorers after Cook would spot New Zealand and some would venture onto land, only two explorers' visits stood out around the end of the 18th century and the beginning of the 19th century. The first was that of French explorer Marc Joseph Marion du Fresne. While the English were exploring the world and the Dutch East India Company continued gaining a trading monopoly on sought-after products, the French were struggling, especially after losing Canada to England during the Seven Years' War. Pairing this with the effects of the French Revolution (1789-1799), France—and, more specifically, the French East India Company—was suffering from financial difficulties. To revive the economy, the French government sponsored a Pacific expedition focused on exploring and creating trade relations. After leaving France in 1771 and sailing from Madagascar to Cape Town, Marion made his way south to the island he self-named Marion Island and Prince Edward Island (just south of South Africa) and continued along the southern coast until arriving in Tasmania. Marion and his crew would be the first Europeans to meet Tasmania's native populations. The ships then continued to New Zealand.

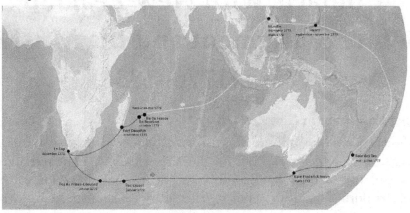

Marion's voyage.

Nweider, CC BY-SA 4.0 <https://creativecommons.org/licenses/by-sa/4.0>, via Wikimedia Commons; Zoomed in; https://commons.wikimedia.org/wiki/File:Trajet_du_Mascarin_et_du_Marquis-de-Castries_entre_1771_et_1773.jpg

In March of 1772, Marion spotted Mount Taranaki, located in the center of New Zealand's North Island's western coast. For the next weeks, he continued sailing north and rounded Spirits Bay (the northernmost coast of New Zealand's North Island) before continuing south along the North Island's eastern coast. All the continuous sailing caused damages to Marion's ships, so the French finally anchored in the Bay of Islands, just off the coast of Moturua Island.

Since the ships had taken quite a beating during the long journey, it would take around five weeks for them to be fixed suitably to travel home. Thus, for the next few months, starting sometime in May, Marion and his companions anchored in New Zealand's Spirits Bay, set up camp, worked on their ships, and communicated with the Māori. Like most European voyages, Marion's ships had many sick passengers, but intelligently, they created a camp solely for the sick on the uninhabited Moturua Island, in addition to two on the mainland. One camp was set up closer to shore, and the other was further from the coast to facilitate gathering materials and cutting wood for rebuilding the ships. Since the French had claimed their Polynesian territory and spent the past decade colonizing Tahiti, many passengers aboard had a base understanding of Tahitian, thanks to the help of Ahutoru, a Tahitian chief who had spent some time in France. Ahutoru was supposed to return home during Marion's Pacific voyage, but he died of smallpox along the way. The French explorer Bougainville, who had originally brought Ahutoru to France, helped take notes on the Tahitian vocabulary and taught Marion and his crew, which would prove indispensable while they were anchored in New Zealand.

While some minor incidents occurred (mostly involving small thefts), according to French reports, the crew got along extremely well with the Māori during their stay, which was until June 1772—about two months after their arrival in New Zealand. A few days after a ceremony that the French believed was held to welcome them, Marion du Fresne and a few other men from his crew were killed by Māori while out fishing. Since none of the men with Marion survived, no one knows what occurred. The following day, Māori attacked another European group ashore, killing more sailors, again for unknown reasons that likely had to do with the events of the day before. It is estimated that twenty-five Europeans died at Māori hands during these violent few days. There is no mention of any Māori fatalities in the Frenchmen's notes. The chief of the Ngare Raumati iwi at the time believed it was Te Kauri, chief of the subtribe Te Hikutuu of the Ngāpuhi iwi, who planned the attack that ended Marion's life, even though he had seemed to be a friend.

It must be noted that all of Marion du Fresne's journals were lost; later, the local Ngare Raumati tribe was overwhelmed by the Ngāpuhi, so no Māori references of the period remain. So, while historians are not entirely sure why Marion was attacked, they have come up with some plausible explanations. Although the French believed they were on good terms with the Māori they encountered, the Māori may not have felt the same way. Some historians theorize that the iwis near Spirits Bay feared that the French would settle permanently, especially after remaining for over five weeks. Since the Ngāpuhi would become violent toward their neighboring tribe, the Ngare Raumati, some historians believe that the Ngāpuhi iwi acted alone. Te Kauri may have organized an attack against the Europeans simply because they were friendly with the Ngare Raumati tribe, who the Ngāpuhi would eventually overrun. It is also very possible that the French encountered various iwis, some of which they were friendly with, similar to the explanation for the convoluted accounts of Cook's time in New Zealand. Though the French could communicate with the Māori, their comprehension was limited, and there is no mention of distinct iwis. This might explain why the attack seemed so sudden—they may have gotten along with one tribe and not another, unknowingly.

After these two smaller battles, the French understood that a war of sorts had begun. With Marion gone, Julien Crozet and his second in command, Ambroise Bernard Marie le Jar du Clesmeur, took control of the ships and began leading the defense to fight off Māori raids. At this point, the Frenchmen still had work to do on their ship before they could leave, and battles with the Māori were becoming destructive. Thus, they organized a strong offensive attack to clear the area and finish their renovations. This counterattack only led to more violent Māori attacks, which would last until mid-July when the ships' reconstructions were finally complete and the French sailed away safely, stopping in the Philippines before returning home.

Effects of Marion's Expedition

It is estimated that during Marion's time in New Zealand, the violent war killed at least 250 Māori. Other than the fatalities, the depth of the effects of the battle on the Māori population is unknown, but it is believed that the French raided Māori villages before they left.

The "Noble Savage"

Marion's expedition had noticeable effects on the European views of the Māori. During the 18th century, writer and philosopher Jean Jacques Rousseau's theories on the "noble savage" were gaining popularity, and in many ways, Marion's visit to New Zealand helped reiterate this belief. The concept of the noble savage is based on John Locke's tabula rasa concept, which states that a person is a sum of their experiences and perceptions. Using tabula rasa as a base, Rousseau famously claimed,

"Man is born free, but is everywhere in chains" (Rousseau, 1895). In other words, a man, even a free man, is not truly free, as he is a slave to the corruption of civilization. Some notable foundations of Rousseau's theories were that all humans have worth (even natives and slaves) and that indigenous populations were freer than free Europeans could ever be. Marion, who was ironically killed by the Māori, was an avid believer in Rousseau's theories of the "uncorrupted savage," which explains how man lives a noble life until corrupted by civilization. Until Marion's death and the Māori battles began, many of the French had developed an appreciation for the lives of the Māori. However, after the violence, this perception changed, and the Māori were once again viewed as dangerous, violent, and untamable. Unlike Cook, who felt that the Māori could be dangerous but believed strongly that New Zealand was worth colonizing, the Frenchmen on Marion's expedition argued that the "dangerous savages" made New Zealand not worth the trouble.

Jules Sébastien César Dumont d'Urville's First Expedition

As mentioned, Marion was not the only notable explorer who reached New Zealand before settlement began. Another French explorer, Jules Sébastien César Dumont d'Urville, also had quite an impact on the Māori population and the global understanding of New Zealand. Like James Cook, Dumont d'Urville helped chart the islands on his three scientific expeditions to New Zealand. In 1823, Dumont d'Urville departed from France with instructions to conduct scientific studies, specifically focused on the flora and fauna of various lands in the Southern Hemisphere. Dumont d'Urville would go on quite the journey, spending about thirty-one months at sea and crossing the equator six times. Aboard *La Coquille*, Dumont d'Urville's ship, were five passengers, two of which were Māori who had spent some time in France. The other passengers were a British missionary and his family, indicating the Europeans' hope to convert indigenous populations they came across. After spending some time on Australia's eastern coast, where they considered creating a settlement, *La Coquille* arrived in New Zealand at the beginning of April 1824.

Like Marion's ship, Dumont d'Urville anchored in the Bay of Islands and was greeted positively by three Māori chiefs. Despite the violence during Marion's expedition, the Europeans and Māori got along peacefully during Dumont d'Urville's two-week stay. Perhaps it was different tribes who met these voyagers, or perhaps other European travelers who had reached New Zealand since Marion's visit had forged peaceful relations with the Māori. Either way, the Māori allowed Dumont d'Urville to station in New Zealand and collect specimens of local plants and bugs. A Māori chief even accompanied the missionary, providing his services as a guide, bodyguard, and translator to ensure the Europeans could communicate safely with Māori tribes without conflict. By the time Dumont d'Urville returned to France in March 1825, he had gathered not only botanical samples from his short stay in New Zealand but also much more information on the Māori's habits, lifestyle, and temperament.

One of the most notable pieces of information Dumont d'Urville's crew gathered from New Zealand was the Māori's version of what caused Marion's death and the ensuing violence. As mentioned, most of the iwi that had close contact with Marion and his crew were overrun by a conflicting tribe. The events had occurred nearly forty years before, yet many Māori had theories about what had happened to cause such destruction after five weeks of peace. Although they were mostly basing their knowledge on rumors and assumptions, the Māori iwis Dumont d'Urville encountered believed that the French were killed for unknowingly engaging in tapu. As mentioned, a tapu, which would inspire the word "taboo" coined by the British during James Cook's expeditions, refers to something considered sacred and inviolable. Essentially, to ignore a tapu is to engage in dishonorable, forbidden behavior (which could be viewed as a sin, such as cheating, in Christian cultures). The Māori population explained that because Marion and his crew could only exchange limited communication with the tribes, a series of misunderstandings likely ensued, leading the French to repeatedly but unknowingly disrespect the Māori's tapu. Perhaps this was done by touching/communicating with someone, cutting down a tree, or visiting a location that was considered tapu. During Dumont d'Urville's visit, the French built upon the European understanding of not only tapu but also general Māori beliefs and traditions.

Dumont d'Urville's Second Expedition to New Zealand

When Dumont d'Urville returned to France from his first expedition to New Zealand, France was considering opening penal colonies. While Dumont d'Urville was mostly just interested in going on another expedition to the Pacific Islands, he proposed New Zealand or Australia as good options for penal colonies to the Minister of Marine. Although the British had claimed both Pacific territories, no true settlement would begin until nearly a decade later. Thus, the French thought they could get away with forming small settlements on the British land. (Of course, these penal colonies would not come to be, as British colonization would begin. France would instead choose French Guiana in the 1850s to house its penal colony.)

Within the year, Dumont d'Urville was approved and funded for another journey across the world. *La Coquille* was fixed up and renamed *Astrolabe*. In April 1826—a little over a year after returning home from his first expedition—Dumont d'Urville and his crew set out for another Pacific voyage. The *Astrolabe* arrived on the West Coast of Australia in October of that year and left from the eastern coast of Australia in December to arrive in New Zealand a month later, in 1827.

While in New Zealand for the second time, Dumont d'Urville had various missions, both assigned and personal. His primary assigned missions were to explain the disappearance of a French expedition in the 1780s that had never come home, conduct further scientific studies, and consider whether New Zealand could be used for a penal colony or settlement. Dumont d'Urville's personal mission was to re-chart the coast of New Zealand, which he felt was not done as precisely by Cook as everyone believed. By February 1827, relics were discovered that explained that the ship that never returned had crashed due to a natural disaster (likely a cyclone). After that discovery, Dumont d'Urville spent nearly three months exploring New Zealand, specifically the western and northern coast of South Island and the eastern coast of North Island. It was during this expedition that many of New Zealand's French-related place names came to be, such as Croisilles Harbour (named for Dumont d'Urville's mother), the French Pass (separating some islands off the northern coast of South Island), and of course, d'Urville Island (just off the northern coast of South Island next to the French Pass), which was named by d'Urville's officers.

Dumont d'Urville was the first European to chart and map New Zealand since James Cook, and he made improvements to Cook's map to create the most accurate map of New Zealand's coast at that time. The *Astrolabe* returned home in March 1829.

After Dumont d'Urville returned to France, the king ordered him to write and publish his scientific notes and studies collected during his second voyage. The books were written by Dumont d'Urville and other scientists and botanists aboard the *Astrolabe,* totaling twelve dense volumes. Interestingly, although Dumont d'Urville spent years at sea and only a brief period in New Zealand, most of his writing focused on New Zealand. The volumes of New Zealand, which also included information on Māori linguistics studies and details of Māori habits and customs, were finished in mid-1835, and mainly focused on botany. They helped to identify and classify hundreds of New Zealand plants and bugs. Much of what we understand today about the Māori population pre-European settlement was confirmed by Dumont d'Urville's lengthy Māori-focused writings.

Although Dumont d'Urville could only focus so much of his volumes on the Māori culture, he was still interested in releasing more of what he had learned about the interesting foreigners. So, he set about writing a historical fiction book, *Voyage Pittoresque Autour du Monde* (English: *Picturesque Voyage Around the World*), which focused more on the Māori. After his death, a different historical fiction was discovered titled *Les Zélandais: Histoire Australienne* (English: *The New Zealanders: Australian History*), which was also focused on the Māori. While the books are certainly fictional (specifically *The New Zealanders,* which follows a Māori chief civilized by European visitors), they help us understand how Dumont d'Urville viewed the Māori. That book's plot follows the chief and his social/family dynamics, Māori warfare, family relations, and communication with fictional missionaries who help to solve conflicts.

Although Dumont d'Urville's books prove that the Māori population were not the savages many Europeans still believed them to be—they had their own values, beliefs, lifestyles, and customs—the fact that the conflict in the books is solved by the missionaries affirms Dumont d'Urville's (and Europeans') general belief that civilized Europeans are superior to indigenous tribes. Dumont d'Urville openly argued against the "noble savage" theory, instead arguing that Māori are not more noble/civilized than Europeans for being uncorrupted but are inferior due to their savage natures. In this translated quote from page 84 of his book *Les Zélandais: Histoire Australienne,* Dumont d'Urville writes:

> "New O happy Civilisation, fruit of the spirit's meditations, fecund mother of enjoyment and bliss. Through you alone, roaming man of long ago, at the mercy of his passions, left his forests, gathered in groups and founded those superb cities which

are evidence of his power and superiority among the beings of creation ... In vain, a few jaundiced philosophes, a few morose critics have tried to deny your excellence and to defend an alleged state of nature which existed only in their disturbed minds. That state of nature is, in reality, only a state of debasement in which man is barely distinguishable from the beasts which surround him, and these same melancholy reformers would themselves blush at being taken back to that state."

There are many takeaways from this passage. First, Dumont d'Urville writes of how humans evolved from those who lived in the forests gathering food into superior humans that built great cities, emphasizing how he believed Māori (and other indigenous populations) to be inferior to Europeans. He goes on to write that some philosophers believe that native tribes are living a more civilized life, but that is an insult to the evolved humans Europeans have become. Those philosophers would not hold these beliefs if they saw those living this way or if they had to live this way.

Though Dumont d'Urville's book is only a work of fiction, these types of writings helped form the European mindset toward the Māori. In the long run, these types of writings proved extremely harmful since they affirmed the belief that the Māori (and other indigenous populations) should be colonized, converted, and "civilized" to evolve.

Interestingly, on page 126 of this book, Dumont d'Urville tries to look at Europeans from the viewpoint of a Māori character. From the perspective of his Māori character who spent time in London, Dumont d'Urville writes:

"I would never finish if I tried to report all their stupid customs, all their absurd practices which I have witnessed in quarters which pride themselves on being so enlightened. In short, where those people are concerned, their time is [so] contrived that every moment of their lives is devoted to imaginary duties and puerile offices, and it leaves them no time to devote to noble reflections of the spirit and to sublime and profound meditations."

In this quote, Dumont d'Urville demonstrates the contradiction that Europeans believed they were enlightened and superior to the Māori, while the Māori spent more time focusing on "enlightenment" by devoting themselves to spiritual thoughts rather than pointless jobs.

While Dumont d'Urville's fictional book only affirmed the views held by most Europeans at the time, it offers an interesting insight into why they treated the Māori (and other indigenous cultures) the way they did.

Diseases Brought to New Zealand by Pre-Settlement Europeans

While some effects of pre-settlement contact were apparent even on Cook's second and third journeys to New Zealand, the effects on the Māori really became apparent in the early 19th century. As in many colonies, when Europeans made contact with the indigenous populations in New Zealand, they brought diseases acquired from months spent not eating properly on unsanitary ships. Although many Europeans would die from these diseases, they eventually built immunities, as living in cities forced them to get used to sickness. Indigenous populations, on the other hand, were living in much more healthy conditions. Their lifestyles were more active, and they had better air and healthier diets. While this was better for their health overall and would mean they could go hundreds of years without developing diseases like the ones that plagued the Europeans, they were not as used to getting sick and had no immunity against the types of diseases brought by Europeans.

Interestingly, most early European visitors to New Zealand successfully contained plagues that killed other indigenous populations. As demonstrated in Marion's expedition, sick people were usually isolated in their own camp away from the Māori. Thus, smallpox and other plagues were not spread throughout New Zealand. Cholera, malaria, yellow fever, and typhus never even reached New Zealand. That said, other very serious diseases, such as measles, typhoid, tuberculosis, influenza, and dysentery, were brought by pre-settlement Europeans. However, much worse than any of those diseases were sexually transmitted diseases, specifically gonorrhea and syphilis, which came to New Zealand after Cook's first visit, confirming that the visiting Europeans had relations with the Māori. Venereal diseases killed the Māori and drastically impacted the birthrate for many years as they increased the chances of stillbirths, infertility, or sterility.

Although some tribes were unlucky, the Māori population was overall successful in avoiding European diseases, especially compared to other indigenous populations. This is likely because Māori iwis were often broken up into subtribes, giving them much smaller numbers than other indigenous groups. Their low-density populations also meant that only small numbers of Māori met with European visitors, which helped contain the diseases. Yet, while there are no exact numbers, it is assumed the Māori population dropped by about 10-30 percent between 1769 and 1840. This has less to do with European diseases and more with other effects of pre-settlement European visits, including the Musket Wars.

The Musket Wars (1807-1842)

As with most wars, there are many different sides to the history. However, most historians believe Hongi Hika, the chief of a Ngāpuhi iwi who lived in the northern area of North Island, started the wars. While the Māori were always in intertribal wars, the Musket Wars would not have been possible without Europeans, who brought muskets to New Zealand, completely changing warfare. According to accounts from the time, by the early 19th century, muskets had been spread throughout New Zealand, and Hongi Hika's tribe had acquired muskets. Yet, considering they were fairly new to the Māori, traditional weapons still won (as when Hongi Hika's tribe was ambushed by a Ngāti Whātua iwi in a typical tribal war around 1807). Although Hongi Hika's tribe had muskets, their reload time took too long, and shots were not always accurate, especially not compared to soldiers who had trained with their weapons of choice. When Hongi Hika's brothers and uncle were killed, he felt the need to get revenge. So, he taught his tribe how to properly use muskets in battle. By 1815, Hongi Hika had gained power in the region, gaining favor with local Māori tribes, and made contact with the European population. He even offered safety to missionary groups and European voyagers in exchange for tools. Considering Hongi Hika was from northern New Zealand, near the Bay of Islands (which he would come to control), it was easy for him to have first access to incoming European ships. While the European voyagers were not willing to trade muskets for protection, they would accept food. So, Hongi Hika began forcing the development of new agricultural techniques and starving his population so that he could exchange food for muskets. Any prisoners of war Hongi Hika captured were put to work as slaves on farms. However, before long, Hongi Hika was capturing more than just Ngāti Whātuas.

Hongi Hika became a destructive force on North Island, destroying dozens of villages from north to central North Island. Thousands of people were killed, and even more slaves were captured. Despite this, Hongi Hika maintained positive relations with the Europeans and even went to England with a missionary. There, he received gifts, most of which he traded for more muskets along the journey home. While some communities avoided destruction using diplomatic tools such as arranged marriages, food/gift offerings, escaping, or joining Hongi Hika's forces, most of the North Island was affected by the Musket Wars. Even by the mid-1820s, Hongi Hika had impacted the southern coast of North Island. Tribes that wanted to defend themselves against Hongi Hika had no other choice but to acquire muskets by any means necessary. Thus, by the end of the Musket Wars, guns became commonplace in New Zealand.

By the late 1820s, most tribes on the North Island had acquired muskets and launched their own campaigns. One such campaign that gained a lot of power was that of the Ngāti Toa tribe, led by Te Rauparaha. Te Rauparaha would become known as the "Napoleon of the South." Just before Hongi Hika died in 1828 from a battle injury, Te Rauparaha moved the Musket Wars into the South Island. Even after Hongi Hika's death, the Musket Wars continued rapidly, as his campaign encouraged most of New Zealand to arm themselves and wage their own campaigns. Before the end of the 1820s, most iwis' pā had been adapted to wartime protection, surrounded with trenches and reinforced with bulletproof walls. Meanwhile, as the Māori tribes engaged in one of New Zealand's most destructive internal wars, European interest in New Zealand only grew. Among the battles of the Musket Wars were European explorers, whalers, merchants, and colonizers looking to form settlements, contributing to New Zealand's convoluted history.

Chapter 7 – The First British Colonization Efforts in New Zealand (1820–1842)

First Temporary European Settlements in New Zealand

While the Musket Wars continued at full force during the first half of the 19th century, European visits to New Zealand did not slow down. New Zealand became home to many temporary European settlements. Most of these consisted of merchants seeking New Zealand's profitable resources, such as timber, seal, whale, or interesting crops they could sell back home. Trade became common between the Māori and European settlers, which explains how the Māori tribes acquired so many muskets during the early years of the Musket Wars. Since England had already begun colonizing Australia in the late 18th century, many of these Europeans in New Zealand had come over from their nearest neighbor. Companies based in Australia began setting up small whaling settlements in New Zealand. Before long, they were joined by other British, French, and American merchants and other hunters and businessmen looking to profit from New Zealand's untapped market. On top of those looking to make a profit, convicts who managed to escape from Australia's penal colony usually hid out in New Zealand, where they sought asylum among these settlements and sometimes even Māori tribes. New Zealand became an unofficial trade center, which is what Dumont d'Urville found when he reached New Zealand on his third expedition.

Dumont d'Urville's Third Expedition to New Zealand

After three voyages, Dumont d'Urville could compare changes in Māori populations from European contact, just as Cook had done. However, the Māori had experienced many more regular European visits, and English colonization had begun. Once again aboard the *Astrolabe*, accompanied by another ship, the *Zelée*, Dumont d'Urville left France in 1837. His crew traveled toward Antarctica before making their way through the Pacific Islands and Australia. Dumont d'Urville would take quite a journey. But once again, before returning home to France, the *Astrolabe* and the *Zelée* stopped in New Zealand in March 1840.

His two ships stopped in Hooper's Inlet, located in the Otago Peninsula on the southeastern coast of New Zealand's South Island. At Hooper's Inlet, they encountered a group of French whalers who informed them of the French whaling settlements set up throughout New Zealand. D'Urville and his crew continued up the east coast until they arrived in Akaroa (located on the east coast in the center of the South Island), where they discovered a thriving French whaling settlement.

The British Decision to Begin Colonization

Despite the British claim on New Zealand, the French had remained interested in the islands since Marion's visit half a century before. This was made clear by the many French whaler settlements. England's decision to begin officially colonizing New Zealand in the 1830s during Dumont d'Urville's third voyage to New Zealand and amid the bloody Musket Wars was not surprising considering the pressure of a French colony and the lawlessness of the merchants who were profiting from New Zealand's resources without taxation or official British approval. Although many Europeans had pleasant communication with New Zealand's tribes before settlement began, the Māori had developed a nasty reputation in Europe, and the islands became known as the "Cannibal Isles." This reputation was, of course, not aided by the Musket Wars, which demonstrated the Māori's advanced training and warfare. It also contributed to the initially slow colonization of New Zealand. This slow British colonization was noted by Dumont D'Urville during his third voyage as he wrote briefly about the annexation of the islands and how the British wanted to conserve the profitable resources for themselves. However, serious settlement efforts began in the 1840s, after the end of the Musket Wars.

The End of the Musket Wars

By the end of the 1830s, the majority of New Zealand's tribes had acquired muskets and had suffered in some ways from the Musket Wars. Most of the Māori population was exhausted after almost four decades of war, with approximately 3,000 battles and raids in the North Island, South Island, and the Chatham Islands. Unlike other colonies, whose indigenous populations decreased from disease and wars with settling Europeans, the Māori population had nearly halved itself before European colonization had even begun, thanks to the Musket Wars. Although the Europeans would eventually force tribes to leave their homes and repopulate, before any settlement, the Musket Wars had caused entire regions of New Zealand to migrate from their homes. The impact of repopulation due to the Musket Wars alone would lead to years of instability in the Māori population and decades of land ownership battles and disagreements. During the decades of battles, regions were burned down and entire villages captured as slaves, which caused irreparable intergenerational damage for some iwis.

Some historians blame not only European muskets for causing the Musket Wars but also European potatoes. While kūmara (sweet potatoes) were traditionally cultivated by men, European potatoes introduced to New Zealand by botanists could be cultivated by men, women, and slaves. Since men were dedicated to kūmara agriculture during the winter months, they could not engage in long battles; typically, warring occurred during the summer, ending in time for the kūmara season to begin. However, with the introduction of the less ritualistic potato, Māori iwis could plant more potatoes and enjoy larger harvests, making more profitable exchanges with Europeans (as in for muskets). Also, wars could last longer.

While in many European retellings of New Zealand's history, especially at the time, the Musket Wars are barely mentioned (and, if they are, it's to describe how violent the Māori population was), the Musket Wars played a massive part in England's ability to colonize New Zealand. The battles made Europeans and their trade indispensable, since only they could provide the muskets needed for tribes to keep up with the violent war.

In exchange for aid in repairing muskets, Māori also allowed Christian missionaries to settle in Māori tribes. While the missionaries supported the end of the Musket Wars, repairing muskets gave them an easy way to gain trust with the Māori and spread the Christian religion and English culture in New Zealand. By the beginning of colonization, many Māori tribes had already begun learning to speak and read English. On top of preaching Christianity, missionaries spoke of how the Māori battles would end and peace could be achieved under a strong royal power like the British Crown. With the extreme violence and destruction of the four-decade war, Māori chiefs were willing to consider all solutions. Missionaries promised that under the British Crown, English leaders would introduce British law, which restricted bloody battles and allowed disagreements to be solved in court. While the idea to end the Musket Wars with the help of the British began in Northern Māori tribes, which had endured the battles for the longest, the movement soon spread, leading to the creation of the Treaty of Waitangi that would allow British settlement and colonization and put an end to the Musket Wars once and for all.

First British New Zealand Resident, Flag, and Declaration of Independence

Although the British waited until the Treaty of Waitangi officially passed to truly begin settling, colonization would have begun regardless. As mentioned before, colonization efforts officially began in the 1830s with England's first resident of New Zealand, James Busby. Busby had spent some time living between Europe and Australia. Accompanied by his family, he was sent to New Zealand by the governor of New South Wales, Australia, with instructions to protect European merchants and settlers from Māori battles and ship back any convicts who had escaped from Australia. Despite the hefty commands, Busby was given very little help from anyone in New South Wales—or England, for that matter. While the Māori Musket Wars continued, everyone was hesitant to begin colonization; thus, Busby was given no military support or power of arrest and absolutely no control over the Māori population.

While Busby was expected to help solve both Māori-European conflicts and issues between British citizens, he had very little experience with conflict control, law enforcement, or Māori culture. Thus, rather than focusing on his assigned instructions, Busby instead began creating a national identity for what would become England's New Zealand. While living in Waitangi, where he had constructed a home for himself and his family, Busby arranged a meeting to decide on a flag for the new nation. He presented three flag options to a group of missionaries,

European settlers, and twenty-five Māori chiefs in March 1834. The flag inspired by one used by the British Church Missionary Society was agreed upon by the voters.

The following year, Busby gathered a similar group of Europeans and chiefs to present a Declaration of Independence for New Zealand, which was essentially a precursor to the Treaty of Waitangi and was recognized by the Crown in 1836. This sudden declaration was most likely in response to the growing French population in New Zealand and the fear that they would attempt to claim the land. The declaration asserted that the Māori would remain independent and protected under the British Crown. Of course, this declaration did little more than prove that England was on its expected trajectory of colonizing New Zealand with only a pretense of consideration for the Māori. In the words of historian Keith Sinclair, the 1836 Declaration of Independence was only a "polite fiction," as Busby would have known that the Māori populations would not remain in control once England arrived, especially considering there was no united national indigenous powerhouse that could take on the Crown. Nonetheless, the Declaration of Independence of 1835 is often seen as the first unifying act between the Māori tribes that had previously existed mostly independent of one another. In the end, the first Declaration of Independence of New Zealand, which promised Māori sovereignty, only got in the way of the signing of the Treaty of Waitangi, as it had to be revoked before the British could assume control of New Zealand.

William Hobson's Arrival in New Zealand

Although Busby proved England would assume control of New Zealand, he did little to maintain control in New Zealand as the bloody Musket Wars continued to wage around him. Thus, in 1837, the governor of New South Wales, Richard Bourke, sent over William Hobson to check on New Zealand and Busby. After having spoken to Busby, various settlers, chiefs, and missionaries, Hobson sent a report back to Bourke explaining that he believed an official colonial governor and trading posts would be the best way to begin settling in New Zealand. Although Busby disagreed, instead pitching that New Zealand should become a protectorate (still in the control of local leaders, aka, the chiefs) rather than a colony, the Crown supported Hobson's report and decided to elect Hobson as the lieutenant governor and British consul in New Zealand. Hobson was instructed to speak to the Māori chiefs who had signed the Declaration of Independence, apologize about revoking the declaration, and begin colonizing New Zealand—but only to obtain and distribute land fairly by way of the Māori. Together, Busby and Hobson began drafting the Treaty of Waitangi to begin England's official colonization of New Zealand.

The Treaty of Waitangi (1840)

Once completed, the Treaty of Waitangi (Te Tiriti o Waitangi), named for the town it would be signed in on the North Island in the Bay of Islands, was translated into Māori by Christian missionary Henry Williams and his son, Edward. To facilitate the spread of the treaty, a meeting was held with several members of the British Crown, Christian missionaries, and nearly 500 Māori in Waitangi on February 5, 1840. The day after the treaty was introduced, February 6, more than forty chiefs signed it.

However, many at the meeting did not believe the treaty would keep England from stealing land, power, and independence from the Māori. Chiefs who did not sign the agreement at the meeting felt that the Māori could handle issues without British aid, as they had done for centuries before. Following the meeting, the treaty was distributed throughout New Zealand, allowing many more Māori chiefs and tribes to view and sign it. Still, the treaty did not reach every region and its many tribes, and it went into effect without the approval of many Māori chiefs. This, of course, differs greatly from the colonization of most other territories, which occurred violently and without any treaty.

The treaty had three articles, none of which mentioned the Musket Wars, but instead the future of New Zealand as a British colony. The first article is slightly confusing as the English version officially decreed that Queen Victoria (and whoever would follow as leader of England) would have full sovereignty over New Zealand. In contrast, the Māori translated version simply gave the English Crown governance. While these words may be synonyms, sovereignty is a much more powerful term than governance. This explains why Māori chiefs may have felt comfortable signing and how they might have felt blindsided in the future. The second article assured that the chiefs would remain in control of their lands (forests, fisheries, villages) and populations. It also specifically mentioned that the Crown would have to go through the Māori chiefs to buy land, unlike in other colonies where they would take what they wanted. The English version of the treaty specifically outlines that Māori chiefs had "exclusive and undisturbed possession" of their properties. The final article of the treaty is the only one identically translated in both versions, and it offers the Māori population rights and protections equal to those of British subjects. This third act, which could prevent future destructive wars, was the only decree the majority of the Māori chiefs were hoping to obtain through this treaty.

First Land Acquirements by the New Zealand Company

Of course, even before the treaty's signing, Māori populations living on New Zealand's North Island had already undergone mass dislocation, which left openings for the British to acquire unpopulated land. Some of the first land trades were made by the New Zealand Company, run by William Wakefield, who was attempting to profit from New Zealand's colonization. Although the company was aware of England's plan to annex New Zealand and disqualify any previous land claims, they believed purchasing land before the Treaty of Waitangi would allow them to resell it at a higher price. Considering land trades with Māori owners would usually take months of discussion since land in the Māori tribes was usually divided among many owners, most of these rushed land trades were made without the acceptance of all the owners. In addition to unlawfully purchasing land without the permission of all its owners, the New Zealand Company was also apparently using false promises—and violence—to acquire land.

By 1840, through less-than-fair methods, the New Zealand Company had acquired land in New Plymouth, Whanganui, and Wellington on the North Island, and in Nelson on the South Island. The New Zealand Company began using propaganda and other dishonesties to sell its property to immigrants looking to begin a life in New Zealand. In May 1840, the Treaty of Waitangi voided most of these land claims; thus, many immigrants arrived in New Zealand cheated, with no land to settle on. Although the company would receive an official royal charter to continue its land purchasing in 1841, the next few years would result in most of its land claims and profits being stripped away. So, the company struggled until its dissolution in 1858.

While land claims purchased through the New Zealand Company were deemed illegitimate, the immigrants still needed somewhere to live, and they quickly began to build a settlement where they disembarked at Port Nicholson, Wellington, on the southern tip of North Island. Soldiers were sent to Wellington, but once they arrived, they found that the settlers were all British citizens looking to help colonize New Zealand; they even suggested Port Nicholson should be New Zealand's capital. While this capital request was denied at the time, Wellington would become the nation's capital in 1865 after decades of debates.

New Zealand's First Capitals

Meanwhile, Hobson and other government officials faced other issues besides the New Zealand Company, including the constant French interest in New Zealand and strategically choosing where to set up the capital and first colonial settlements. Hobson had spent months before and after the Treaty of Waitangi meeting with missionaries and surveying land that could be purchased and used for a capital. It seemed to be decided that the capital city would be around Waitematā Harbour. However, just after the treaty's signing in February, Hobson suffered from a stroke while surveying land, which would take him a month to recover from. With Hobson's health issues, the government decided to set up a temporary capital in the Bay of Islands town of Okiato, just outside of Russell, which had been their home base during the Treaty of Waitangi discussions.

Once the treaty had been signed and Hobson recovered, Māori chiefs from Ōrākei, in the Waitematā Harbour, came to offer their land for the capital city in exchange for protection from a rival iwi and European immigration. The British gradually built up Russell, intending to move the capital to the Waitematā Harbour. However, the move was advanced by the arrival of the French. In July and August of 1840, French ships filled with immigrants arrived with the intention of creating a permanent settlement. Since the Treaty of Waitangi had only just passed, many were unaware of England's official claim on New Zealand. Hobson felt that creating a proper capital city would demonstrate that England's land claim was legitimate and that it was too late for other nations to claim land.

The Waitematā Harbour area (renamed Auckland, after Lord Auckland), was conveniently located between popular harbors. It had also already been mostly depopulated by the Musket Wars. Thus, the New Zealand government began proceedings to make Auckland the new capital, including claiming the land and raising the flag in September, sending settlers in October, and officially moving all government officials and their families there in February 1841. Although Auckland would not remain New Zealand's capital for long, it served as a base for England's government in the colony's early days and would eventually become New Zealand's most populous city.

Meanwhile, as Auckland transformed into New Zealand's second capital in a matter of months, immigrants continued to settle in Port Nicholson, Wellington. As a newer city, in comparison, Auckland was less populated, had fewer amenities and jobs, and was more expensive to live in. Settlers in Port Nicholson sent petitions to the British Crown demanding a capital change; however, by this time, government establishments had begun to form in Auckland, making it more complicated to move again. By the end of 1840, the *New Zealand Government Gazette* had released its first papers, with one issue based on South Island and one in Auckland for the North Island. The location of the government house was decided in 1840, and construction of the massive mansion was completed at the beginning of 1841—perfect timing for the government officials to move in. Hobson himself moved into the government house in March 1841, officially regarded as the date the capital changed to Auckland. Also in 1841, the Supreme Court of New Zealand was founded in Auckland. Construction of the court was finished the following year.

Chapter 8 – The First Decades of British Settlement

New Zealand Officially Becoming a Colony

While England's early colonization efforts legitimized its claim on New Zealand to other European nations, it was not a focus of the Crown until the Treaty of Waitangi. Until 1841, New Zealand was not even its own colony but a part of New South Wales (Australia), where Busby, Hobson, and most of its other government officials had been sent from. While Busby's flag of New Zealand had been raised throughout the nation, New Zealand only legally separated from Australia's colony in 1841, when it earned its status as a British Crown colony entitled to its own government, constitution, and financing. Thus, Hobson's status was elevated from lieutenant governor to governor of New Zealand.

However, a new colony means a distinct set of issues. For New Zealand, many conflicts would arise from the papers that legitimized its status: the Treaty of Waitangi. Hobson's promise to protect the Māori convinced many unsure chiefs to sign the treaty; however, most conflicts in New Zealand's colonial history return to the poor translation of the word "sovereignty," which led chiefs to believe that the Māori would remain autonomous. In the early 1840s, the famous mistranslation came to light as the Māori felt that land was being unfairly acquired by the British. The government did little to help, as the Māori were under the sovereignty of the Crown. After Hobson's death in 1842, his successor Robert FitzRoy, struggled to maintain the peace between the Māori and

Europeans.

The Wairau Massacre

As mentioned, in the 1830s, the New Zealand Company had acquired land from the Māori through many dishonest methods, and many of the land claims should have been voided after the Treaty of Waitangi was passed. This became apparent in the New Zealand Company's first settlement in Port Nicholson, Wellington, and in Nelson, on the northern tip of South Island. While the Māori were upset by the land claims they viewed as invalid, the British were also disgruntled, as many had immigrated from England only to find the land they were promised did not exist. This was especially frustrating to the Europeans, who did not understand why they needed the approval of the Māori to inhabit the land, as most other British colonies had begun settling without indigenous approval.

One of the reasons for the confusion regarding land sales was that the New Zealand Company purchased much of its land from the Ngāti Toa, which had been at the forefront of the violent campaigns during the Musket Wars. While the Ngāti Toa tribe may have been inhabiting the area of Nelson during the Musket Wars, the tribes in the northern area of South Island did not feel that the Ngāti Toa had any claim to the land. Chief of the Ngāti Toa, Te Rauparaha, one of the most powerful leaders during the Musket Wars, apparently signed land over to Wakefield of the New Zealand Company. However, Te Rauparaha, who signed the Treaty of Waitangi and greatly opposed European settlement, argued he never signed over land to Wakefield or any other European. Of course, it was hard to trust Te Rauparaha, who aided in destroying New Zealand and dislocating the Māori.

As mentioned, the 500 immigrants who had arrived in Nelson (and the over 1,000 more on their way to the land) had nowhere else to go and stayed despite the conflict. While the Māori tribes near Nelson profited initially from food trades, they had expected that the act which protected their land claim in the Treaty of Waitangi would prevent permanent settlement; however, the New Zealand Company remained.

The situation worsened in 1843 when the settlers began surveying the nearby land for fertile plains they could farm and wanted to develop the Wairau Valley. Te Rauparaha and other Māori chiefs argued that, even if the company's claim to Nelson was valid, the Wairau Valley was seventy kilometers away and was not included in the (debatably) agreed-upon purchase. Despite the Ngāti Toa ordering the company to leave the Wairau Valley out of their settlement plans, a few months later, William Wakefield and his brother resumed plans to begin settlement there, hoping profitable farmlands would convince the Crown to legitimize their land claims. Frustrated, the Ngāti Toa burned down the settlers' first establishments and temporary shelters and once again ordered the British to leave the area. The Company decided to defy the Māori wishes and arrest Chief Te Rauparaha and his nephew Te Rangihaeata for arson. In June 1843, around fifty Europeans, including William Wakefield's brother Arthur Wakefield and Nelson's chief constable Henry Thompson, came to Tuamarina River to arrest the arsonists, where they were met by roughly 100 prepared, armed Māori. An accidental European musket shot led to a violent battle that killed approximately thirteen Europeans and two Māori. The rest of the outnumbered Europeans were captured, and since one of the Māori killed in the battle was Te Rangihaeata's wife, Arthur Wakefield and Henry Thompson were executed. The others were set free.

The Wairau Incident (known to Europeans as the Wairau Massacre) shocked settlers. When Robert FitzRoy arrived in New Zealand at the end of 1843 to take over Hobson's governorship, most of the colony was calling for action against the violent Ngāti Toa responsible for the execution. FitzRoy, in his first major decision as leader, decided not to punish the Te Rauparaha or his tribe for the executions, whether because the government believed the Māori were against the New Zealand Company or he simply did not want to spend the money to take military action against the Ngāti Toa. Although the Māori and Europeans had entered the mid-19th century with seemingly good relations, one incident was all it would take to change the precarious peace that had been established. The New Zealand Company demanded FitzRoy be replaced. After similar incidents between Māori and Europeans continued, FitzRoy was recalled in 1845.

Governor George Grey

While Fitzroy inherited New Zealand in a time of economic and social difficulties, he passed on an even more distressed colony to his successor, George Grey. Unlike Fitzroy and even Hobson before, Grey was prepared for the struggles he'd encounter during his short stints as governor of New Zealand. Although he'd only hold the position between the years 1845-53 and then again between 1861-1868, he is still considered one of New Zealand's most famous, influential, and important figures. Before becoming the governor of New Zealand, George Grey always had an interest in indigenous affairs and far-off lands, which explains why he offered to lead an expedition to Australia at only twenty-five years old. After two voyages to Australia, Grey wrote a paper about colonial relations with indigenous peoples, which impressed the British Crown enough to promote him to governor of South Australia. At the time, South Australia's colony was suffering from similar social and financial problems as New Zealand. While Grey improved the latter issue, his five-year governorship did little to improve indigenous relations. However, the British Crown would quickly allow Grey to try again since Fitzroy's recall required a governor with some experience to transform New Zealand. After Fitzroy's governorship, the British Crown realized New Zealand needed further funding if it was going to succeed. Therefore, Grey had a leg up on his predecessor, with access to a larger budget and troops. Both were necessary, especially considering that the Northern War, also known as the Flagstaff War, had just begun as Grey arrived in New Zealand.

The Northern War

Years after Ngāpuhi chief Hongi Hika had started the Musket Wars, the northern tribe of Ngāpuhi made history again when Maketū Wharetōtara, the son of its new chief Ruhe, apparently killed five Europeans. In the 1840s, the future that many of the Māori chiefs had feared when signing the Treaty of Waitangi began to come true as land was taken away and working Māori were treated unfairly. Sixteen-year-old Maketū Wharetōtara had been working for a European family that had apparently abused him, a common occurrence during this time, which led Maketū to kill his employer and their family (including the young children). Maketū Wharetōtara returned to his home Ngāpuhi village, which led the nearby Europeans to fear an uprising. Although the local police magistrate refused to get involved, Hōne Heke, another powerful Ngāpuhi chief, defended Maketū. In the end, the young boy surrendered with the support of his father and his Maketū Ngāpuhi village. After being found guilty at trial in 1842, Maketū was not only the first Māori to be punished by British rule but the first person hung by British law in New Zealand.

The execution of Maketū Wharetōtara is considered by many to be the point when many Māori realized they had and would continue to lose their independence under English rule. In the convoluted years that followed the execution (which included the Wairau Massacre and other battles), Ngāpuhi chief Hōne Heke, who had defended Maketū's actions, decided the Māori needed to fight back before they lost their chance to reclaim their land. However, not all the Māori wanted to fight the English presence. Especially in the years following the devastating Musket Wars, many northern tribes wanted to avoid allowing another Ngāpuhi chief to take too much power. The Northern War is complicated because it was not simply the Māori against the English, but the Hōne Heke Ngāpuhi tribe against the English, who had allied with another group of Ngāpuhi.

After the signing of the Treaty of Waitangi, the flag created by Busby, in alliance with Māori chiefs that had come to represent the United Tribes of New Zealand, was replaced by the British Union Jack flag. The flagstaff in Kororāreka (Russell) symbolized English superiority; thus, it became the target of Heke's rebellion. The Ngāpuhi, led by Hōne Heke, cut down the flagstaff three times before it was replaced by an iron-clad, blockhouse, guard-protected flagstaff. Hōne Heke created a distraction that allowed his Ngāpuhi to down the flagstaff a fourth time, leading to an all-out war that destroyed the settler town of Kororāreka. While a few dozen were killed from each side, tens of thousands of dollars of damage were done to the new establishments that had been built. In response, more military was called upon, and more offensive attacks were used, resulting in the destruction of multiple Māori pā and the death of hundreds of Māori. Over the months of war, the Māori learned how to increase the defense of their pā with walls that could withstand firepower.

Most of this fighting occurred during Fitzroy's governorship, and when Grey took over the position, he was determined to end the war. Grey demanded and received a force of over a thousand men, nearly triple the number of Māori soldiers. In January of 1846, Grey's military successfully overtook the Ruapekapeka pā. Lacking resources, Heke and his ally Kawiti were forced to surrender their fight, leading Grey to revel in his first official victory as governor of New Zealand. Although Grey did not address the issues that led to the Northern War in the first place, a sort of uneasy peace between the Māori and the European settlers was attained.

The New Zealand Wars

The Wairau Conflict and the Northern War are both examples of battles in the New Zealand Wars, a series of conflicts between various Māori tribes and the British colonial government (which often allied with different Māori tribes). While the battles were mostly unrelated, they all came down to conflicts about land and Māori losing their power.

New Zealand Pre-Constitution

Between the beginning of the New Zealand Wars, which would last until 1872, and the governorship of the influential George Grey, the 1840s-1860s would mark a significant turning point in New Zealand's history. After the Northern War ended, Grey sent out many orders to bring peace to New Zealand and give the new settlers a chance at successful growth. One of these actions was the military arrest of Ngāti Toa chief Te Rauparaha, accused of illegally supplying weapons to Māori tribes revolting against British rule. Te Rauparaha was imprisoned without a trial. Grey also facilitated the purchase of Māori land for European settlements, mainly through his lieutenant Donald McLean. Uprisings were prevented, and rebellions were squashed throughout both islands. Once Hōne Heke's flagstaff rebellion was thwarted, a temporary but fragile peace was attained in New Zealand. While most of the ethnic conflicts had been quelled, New Zealand was still in a state of economic distress. However, rather than focusing on the economy, Grey decided (with pressure from the British Crown) it would be best to pay attention to New Zealand's lack of government, laws, and establishments.

In 1846, while Grey tackled the New Zealand Wars, the British Crown issued the New Zealand Constitution Act, which proposed that a representative government be formed. New Zealand was not a priority, especially compared to other more profitable colonies, and the Crown understood that the United Kingdom's government would not be able to reasonably govern New Zealand from so far away. At this time, there were around 13,000 colonists in New Zealand, many of whom were sending complaints to the British Crown that their needs were being overlooked in the face of Māori issues. With a representative government, the colonists could handle their own conflicts and complaints without constantly complaining to the British Crown. However, proving their point, Governor George Grey argued that a representative government may benefit the settlers but would lead to larger issues, as it would not respect the rights of the Māori, who were still the majority of the population in New Zealand. Grey convinced the Crown to postpone representational government for five years while he began writing his own constitution that would better suit the needs of the mixed population.

Although the ethnic and economic struggles had improved by the late 1840s, the end of the decade was marked by the most political agitation New Zealand had ever seen. This is not much of a surprise considering its government was only created a decade before. However, the dissatisfaction the settlers of New Zealand had with their new government resembled that of an older society that had undergone decades of frustration and disappointment. Dissatisfaction was common in every settlement but that of the capital, Auckland. Hundreds of letters were sent to Grey demanding and pleading for representative government. Yet, George Grey remained in power, using the letters as inspiration to draft the New Zealand Constitution Act of 1852, which he hoped would address the concerns of the Māori population and the demands of the settlers. While most leaders who held back self-government are viewed as authoritarian and cruel, many still see Grey as New Zealand's best governor. This is mostly because he did not want New Zealand to be a dictatorship; he simply wanted to delay self-government until Māori conflicts were solved, assimilation strategies were established, and fair land policies were in place. While George Grey lost his settler support, he remained on good terms with the Māori population and the British Crown and was even knighted in 1848.

At the start of the 1850s, the economic issues mostly ended when gold was discovered in Australia. New Zealanders had the advantage of being able to reach Australia before other Europeans. This, in combination with the massive growth in Australia's population creating a need for New Zealand's agriculture and products, led to an economic boom in New Zealand.

New Zealand Constitution Act 1852

In January 1853, the New Zealand Constitution (of 1852) came into effect, of which George Grey was the chief author. The primary changes introduced in this constitution were the establishment of a representative government through provincial and national assemblies. Under the new constitution, New Zealand was divided into six provinces: Auckland, New Plymouth (Taranaki), Wellington, Nelson, Canterbury, and Otago. This would not be the final division of the land, as it would eventually be divided further into ten provinces; however, it was a change from the 1841 provincial division of New Zealand that came after the Treaty of Waitangi. In 1841, New Zealand had been split into three provinces: New Ulster, which included the northern two-thirds or so of the North Island north of the Patea River; New Munster, which was the entire South Island and the bottom third of the North Island; and New Leinster, which included Stewart Island/Rakiura.

Each of the six provinces had an elected superintendent and a provincial council. Although the government was now representative, there was still a central government which was now extended to include a two-part legislature made up of a General Assembly (which was nominated by the Crown and would act as the Legislative Council) and a House of Representatives. The House of Representatives was voted in by men over twenty-one who owned land (or rented valuable property), and representatives would hold their positions for five years. Although Māori owned land, Māori land was usually owned communally; therefore, they were mostly exempt from voting. Eventually, in 1867, four Māori were given parliamentary seats, but this small representation did little to sway any decision in a Parliament of seventy-six members. Since there was no Māori sector of the government, it was up to Grey and any governor who followed to keep Māori affairs in mind.

The New Zealand Parliament held its first meeting in 1854. But, since the colony had technically not achieved self-government, the event had very little consequence other than introducing future men of influence to one another. By the time New Zealand held its first government meetings under the new constitution, Grey's term as governor had ended, and he was replaced with a provisional governor, Col. Robert Henry Wynyard. In Wynward's nearly two years as governor, the demand for a responsible government rapidly increased.

Māori Affairs in the 1850s

The population of non-Māori New Zealanders, who came to be known as Pākehā, had already greatly affected Māori life. But, beginning in 1850, the Pākehā impact would be even more dramatic as the settlements began to grow rapidly. With the Australian gold rush and the eventual New Zealand gold rush, New Zealand's population was growing rapidly, increasing the pressure on the Māori to sell their land. While in 1850 the population of New Zealand is estimated to have been about 75 percent Māori, by 1858, there were more Europeans than Māori in New

Zealand. Although settlement had increased in the 1850s, this demographic change had more to do with the impact of settlers than the number of incoming Europeans.

Compared other indigenous populations, the Māori tribes had mostly been spared from the spread of fatal diseases and deadly land wars with Europeans until this point. But their fortune was beginning to change. As more settlers arrived in New Zealand, the Māori's immune systems were constantly tested as pneumonia, viral diseases, typhoid fever, tuberculosis, and various respiratory infections spread. Although hospitals had been set up for the Māori by churches and settler communities, between 1840 to 1891, the Māori death rate was higher than ever. Meanwhile, as the Māori attempted to fight off disease, legal and illegal land sales were forcing dislocation, significantly impacting tribes that had lived in a specific region with a lifestyle that fit their land for generations. As Māori tribes were moved or forced to integrate with their new neighboring settler communities, everything changed—from diet and water supplies to houses and sanitation. All these factors, combined with the decrease in birth rates, cut the Māori population in half, with the largest decline between 1840 and 1878.

Governor Thomas Gore Browne

In 1855, England replaced the provisional governor Col. Robert Henry Wynyard with Thomas Gore Browne, whose military experience could not prepare him for the mess he inherited in New Zealand. Although Grey had temporarily established peace in his government, tensions were high when Browne finally arrived. During the 1850s, the demand for self-government had skyrocketed, and to maintain order, Wynyard had allowed the provincial institutions to make most of the decisions, a pattern Browne would also follow during his governorship. Of course, this meant that the Māori's fears and Grey's prediction had come true: the settlers would have little respect for Māori land claims as they grew their settlements and focused on the economy.

Since each province was mostly self-governing during the 1850s, it spent money on different establishments. Canterbury and Otago, which make up a large portion of South Island, had very small Māori populations, especially in comparison to North Island. Therefore, they could spend more money on immigration and education. In North Island, settlers had more trouble expanding as the larger Māori population meant land had to be bought. Their expansion depended on not only their economy and budget but also the Māori's willingness to sell. The Māori, fearing the loss of their small amount of control, rarely sold desirable land. By the beginning of the 1850s, most of the land the Māori were willing to sell had been bought. And with Māori settlements between European settlements, it would take decades until roads. With no governor to look out for the Māori interests, the tribes were left almost completely unrepresented in government affairs. So, as the land ran out in the 1840s, the self-governing provinces of the 1850s presented a solution: land acquisition with proper Māori approval.

The Māori King Movement

By the mid-1850s, any harmony established between the Māori and the settlers had deteriorated. In 1856, after nearly two decades of demanding, the New Zealand Parliament finally received a responsible government. While this was a win for the settlers, who could finally elect representatives with actual power, the governor had lost his absolute power. This was a loss for the Māori, as the governor was the only branch of government looking out for the concerns of the Māori people.

The North Island, with its larger Māori population, struggled to overcome the ever-growing conflicts once a responsible government was achieved. By 1860, 80 percent of New Zealand's North Island was still owned by Māori tribes, forcing the Pākehā population to settle on the coast, with little room for expansion. While the Māori population did use some of the land for farming, as commercial farms owned and run by Māori were very popular at this time, much of the land was unused—at least in the eyes of the settlers. The Māori had many reasons they didn't want to sell their "wasteland," as it came to be known by Pākehās, whether for sacred reasons or just the fear that settlers would gain control of the island. The Pākehās were becoming increasingly frustrated by the lack of expansion room, and the Parliament rightfully believed New Zealand would not grow economically, politically, or socially if it could not grow spatially. So, the Parliament began putting additional pressure on Māori to sell their land. With no autocratic governor looking out for their interests, many Māori felt the need to select a leader of their own. While the Māori communities had always been connected, each tribe had its own chief. In the 1850s, the Māori of northern New Zealand began considering a single figure who would represent them in land conflicts with the settlers and look out for their general needs in a way the European governors never could. Thus, was the creation of the Kīngitanga, or the King Movement.

The First Māori King and Opposition to the King Movement

While the northern Waikato region of New Zealand's North Island decided to select a king to defend their land against the growing settler population, not all Māori tribes were on board. Many chiefs felt they should not have to put their power in the hands of another, and many tribes who did not feel connected to the Waikato chief chosen to be king decided not to follow the Kīngitanga. Yet, in 1858, with the support of the Waikato and Maniopoto tribes, Te Wherowhero became the first Māori King, known as King Pōtatau I. In the nearby Taranaki province (just south of the Waikato tribe), where land shortage was also a major issue, a different leader took command. Without any royal status, the chief of the Te Ātiawa tribe, Wiremu Kīngi (Te Rangitāke), would become a powerful force against settler land purchases. Of course, many Māori wanted to continue to profit from land sales, which the Māori king and Wiremu Kīngi directly opposed, giving tribes another reason to not support the King Movement or a chief in autocratic power.

While both Māori movements had similar goals, they remained separate, as those in the Taranaki province could not support one leader having that much mana (power). While King Pōtatau I tried to unite the Māori tribes during his reign, most chiefs and tribes refused to support him. Regardless of the lack of Māori backing, King Pōtatau I established an unbroken dynasty, which continued with his own son Tāwhiao. Despite a lack of support from the nearby Māori tribes and opposition from the Pākehās, King Tāwhiao managed to keep the Māori King Movement alive by leading his followers in exile to the northernmost tip of New Zealand's North Island, which is now known as King Country. To this day, New Zealand has a king who is part of the unbroken Te Wherowhero royal dynasty.

Wars and Māori-Pākehā Conflicts

With so many opposing opinions all concentrated in New Zealand's North Island, it is no surprise that the 1860s were marked by another period of conflict. When Governor Gore Browne attempted to buy land from a Taranaki sub-chief, ignoring the veto of land sales set by Wiremu Kīngi, miscommunication led to an intense battle. When peace was finally made in 1861, Browne decided it would be necessary to invade

Waikato and dismantle the King Movement to prevent similar wars. However, his term ended that year, and he was replaced by the popular George Grey, back in New Zealand to serve a second term as governor. Grey demanded that the Māori near Waikato pledge allegiance to the British queen. When they refused the ultimatum, he decided to carry out the plans set forth by his predecessor and begin the decade-long Waitara block. While the British Crown had Grey reappointed in hopes that he would bring peace to New Zealand, George Grey ordered 12,000 imperial troops to invade Waikato in July 1863. The battle would continue for several months, but as the Māori force paled compared to Grey's troops, the colonial government emerged victorious, allowing them to claim Māori land.

Meanwhile, as Grey focused on aggressively trying to dismantle the Māori King Movement, warring spread through North Island. As tribes struggled to survive in constant conflicts, different Māori leaders came and went. Not all were political chiefs focused on preserving Māori land. One example of this new wave of Māori leaders is Te Ua Haumēne, who created a religion known as Pai Mārire (Hauhau), which combined Māori religion with Jewish and Christian beliefs. Those who supported Pai Mārire engaged in many religious conflicts in the 1860s against the Pākehā government—and against Māori. When Te Kooti, a warrior who also created a religion based on Christianity (Ringatū), outwardly opposed Te Ua Haumēne, the two groups entered religious wars. In 1872, Te Kooti was given sanctuary by King Tāwhiao, ending most of the religious warring.

The Māori Population in the 1870s

Most of the conflicts fought during the mid-19th century seemed to end by the beginning of the 1870s. Once again, New Zealand found itself in a fragile state of peace. Although the warring had mostly stopped, Māori resentment towards European settlers deepened. By 1860, 65 percent of Māori land had transferred into settler hands, a number worsened by the 1862 Native Land Act, which legalized and facilitated Māori-settler land exchanges. Through war in the 1870s and displacement due to the increasing European settler population and the spread of diseases, the Māori population steadily decreased, as it had since the 1840 Treaty of Waitangi. By 1896, the Māori population would reach a low of 42,000, which looked bleak compared to the nearly

700,000 settlers of European descent recorded that year. It became a common belief that it would not be long before there were no more Māori in New Zealand—which, after years of conflict, was not a bad thing in the eyes of the settlers. As scientist Alfred Newman said, "The disappearance of the race is scarcely subject for much regret. They are dying out in a quick, easy way, and are being supplanted by a superior race" (Newman, 1881, quoted by Pool and Kukutai 2018). This quote reflects not only the miserable Māori situation in the 19th century but also the views of many settlers toward those who had inhabited New Zealand before them.

Raupatu

Although settlers had taken land from Māori tribes since their arrival in New Zealand, land confiscations (known as Raupatu in Māori) became generationally devastating after the 1860s. While some land was claimed during war, even Māori tribes who had pledged their allegiance to the British queen and fought on the imperial side against defensive Māori tribes had land confiscated. Land was confiscated not only for settler communities but also for military settlements. By 1879, Parihaka, located centrally on New Zealand's North Island, became the home to the Raupatu opposition movement. Before their imprisonment in 1881, two Māori chiefs, Te Whiti-o-Rongomai and Tohu Kākahi, encouraged frustrated Māori to destroy new constructions in soon-to-be Pākehā settlements to claim back their land.

New Zealand's Gold Rush

As in previous decades, the wars that had plagued New Zealand's North Island since European settlement had taken a toll on the region's economy. This was especially obvious when comparing North Island to South Island, which had experienced massive economic growth. In 1852, gold was discovered on New Zealand's North Island near Coromandel. Although some settlers heard the news and began searching, New Zealand's gold rush, mostly focused in South Island, wouldn't truly begin until a decade after the first discovery of gold. In 1861, a man named Gabriel Read discovered gold in Otago, on South Island, which brought thousands of miners and settlers there. Over the 1860s, gold would also be discovered along the west coast and again near Coromandel, which helped to cement that the New Zealand gold rush had begun. This was timed perfectly, as the Australian gold rush had begun to slow down, allowing miners to quickly relocate to Australia's closest neighbor to continue chasing their fortune. Alongside European miners came a large Chinese population, which greatly contributed to New Zealand's developing culture.

The Economy in South Island

Unlike other gold rushes, few miners got rich in New Zealand. While gold collectively mined in New Zealand helped develop an economy, the settlements and businesses surrounding the gold mining would establish South Island's profitable economy. Although the capital, businesses, and most populous cities had all been on North Island, after 1860, South Island became home to most of New Zealand's Pākehā population and the colony's source of wealth. North Island would take years to recover from war, and it would not be until the beginning of the 20th century that its population and economy would finally overtake South Island again.

The European Population of New Zealand

After 1860, the population of New Zealand grew at exponential rates. New Zealand attracted a predominantly young male population planning to mine, forcing the government to entice unmarried females to immigrate. Schemes to balance out the genders would continue well into the 20th century, proven by posters released in England by the New Zealand High Commissioner's office in London in 1913, which said: "New Zealand wants domestic Servants. Rich Country, Fine Climate, Good Wages, Work Waiting." Schemes were also created to attract older, educated populations.

Sir Julius Vogel

While the late 1850s and early 1860s had proven extremely profitable for many regions of New Zealand, the end of the 1860s marked the end of the gold rush and decreased demand and prices for previously profitable exports such as wool. In 1870, Julius Vogel, New Zealand's colonial treasurer at the time, offered a development strategy that involved borrowing British funds to develop the colony. This policy had already been attempted on a smaller scale in some provinces of New Zealand in 1867 and ended in disaster. Borrowed money had been carelessly spent while the colony was financially prospering, leaving it in debt by the time of the economic depression. This led to the creation of laws that prohibited overseas borrowing. However, when the gold rush reached a sudden halt in 1867, both New Zealand's islands (specifically, South Island) had entered a financial crisis so bad that the laws prohibiting overseas borrowing were repealed by 1870.

Vogel believed that New Zealand had untapped economic potential but simply lacked the capital and labor necessary to be properly developed. Vogel's plan could be split into three main plans of action. First, as the wars in North Island ended, Vogel insisted funds should be spent purchasing Māori land that had been previously protected. Second, British immigrants should be encouraged to move to New Zealand, with their travel fees subsidized by the English government, to help grow the labor force and businesses in New Zealand. Finally, British-borrowed funds would be invested in constructing infrastructure to connect the isolated colony through railways, bridges, and roads and to the rest of the world through ports and telegraph lines. By 1873, Vogel had taken the position of prime minister of New Zealand, allowing him to execute his plans with little opposition. The responsibility of construction would be in the hands of the central government rather than the provinces, which had previously overseen colonizing their regions by growing the population and economy. Of course, the provincial governments did not favor losing their power. After a few years of debates, in 1876, Vogel abolished provincial governments altogether. Through an overall smooth transition in all provinces but Otago, provincial affairs were transferred to delegates in the General Assembly rather than individual provincial governments.

One of Vogel's more ambitious plans was to connect New Zealand's previously isolated towns through 1,600 kilometers of railways in nine years to encourage settlement and the colonial economy. In 1870, before Vogel's construction began, there were only seventy-four kilometers of train tracks in New Zealand. But, by 1880, there were around 2,000 kilometers of rail lines, surpassing Vogel's original proposal. Vogel challenged New Zealand's development model, claiming that New Zealand's progress would only come if the settlers worked together as a single nation rather than individual, remote regions as they had been before. Advancement also meant that the children of New Zealand needed to be educated, and the Māori could no longer be treated so poorly that they'd be driven to war—which would destroy what Vogel was attempting to build. The 1870s marked a period of the massive loss of Māori land and a decrease in the Māori population, mostly due to the mass British immigration to New Zealand. While the country still has a long way to go in Pākehā-Māori affairs, some improvements were made in the 1870s. For example, missionary schools were dismantled and replaced with native schools to educate the Māori population.

Meanwhile, in 1877, the Education Act was also implemented to help develop a network of public schools in New Zealand for the Pākehā population. By 1900, New Zealand would have a population of around 500,000—nearly double what it was before Vogel's administration.

New Zealand's Economic Depression 1879-1895

While Vogel is seen as an innovative leader who helped transform New Zealand during his short time in government, not all his programs were as successful as the railway construction, immigration, and development of educational programs, giving him somewhat of a controversial reputation. Although the money invested in New Zealand had been invested wisely in the necessary infrastructure to develop the colony, most of the funds were used on public works that would not show a short-term economic return. For example, constructing means of transportation improved New Zealand's long-term development but didn't immediately increase economic productivity to repay the massive loans borrowed from England. Thanks to Vogel, New Zealand's debt had grown exponentially.

Although construction jobs had been created, British settlers had trouble making ends meet, especially those who had bought land in New Zealand before the price and demand of farm products decreased. The rise of private lending agencies allowed immigrants to acquire land they could no longer afford, as jobs had no security and interest rates rose exponentially. Immigrants continued to arrive in New Zealand; however, there were not enough jobs to accommodate the doubled population, and unemployment rates were higher than ever.

So, despite the growth and development initiated by Vogel, New Zealand's optimism for the future was replaced in 1879 by a disastrous financial depression that would last until the end of the 19th century. Many blamed Vogel's borrowing strategy, which didn't create income to repay the loans and failed to prepare the colony for what would happen when the money dried up. Vogel had not established welfare or insurance of any kind to protect the immigrants he had promised jobs for on arrival. Thus, women and children were forced into horrendous working conditions to help support the men. As women were forced to take on more responsibility, which became especially necessary as alcoholism rates rose in men, women began their fight for suffrage.

While the end of the 19th century was difficult for New Zealanders, some positives did come out of the struggles. After spending most of the

1880s and early 1890s working in poor conditions and revolution, New Zealand women earned their right to vote in 1893, making New Zealand the first country to allow women to vote in national elections. In the 1880s, the minister of lands, William Rolleston, realized New Zealand's land was mostly in the hands of a few large, wealthy elites. While these farms offered jobs to the unemployed and fed the people of New Zealand, the monopoly on pastoral land was not helping the economic depression. To solve this, Rolleston introduced tenant farming, which allowed lower-income farmers to rent land from wealthy landowners. Although there wasn't a huge need for farm products in New Zealand since the wealthy farm owners already met the demand, the tenant movement was perfectly timed with the rising demand for farm products around the world—and, in 1882, the creation of safe shipment of frozen goods abroad using refrigeration. What began with frozen meat shipments to England eventually spiraled into frozen butter, cheese, and other farm products around the world.

The Liberal Era (1891–1912)

In 1890, a massive change came to New Zealand's politics when plural voting, which allowed landowners to vote in every electorate zone where they owned land, was finally revoked. After a decade of economic struggles, nationwide strikes, unionizing, and women's suffrage, New Zealanders wanted a change. In 1890, the people of New Zealand eligible to vote voted in New Zealand's first political party, the Liberal Party. (Gradually, during the Liberal's two-decade governorship, the conservative opposition would form its own party in 1908 known as the Reform Party.) The Liberal Party tried to focus on filling the gaps that became obvious during the depression, such as New Zealand's horrific work conditions, the need for income-based tax brackets, and the lack of welfare. While John Ballance led the Liberal Party initially, he passed away in 1893, two years after becoming prime minister, and was replaced by the more notable Richard John Seddon, known as "King Dick."

Richard John Seddon

Prime Minister Seddon, following the path of his predecessor, focused on buying land, mostly from Māori landowners, which was then leased to farmers. Tenant farming not only helped create a demand for New Zealand farm products worldwide but also helped develop the islands, which were still isolated and rural at the end of the 19th century. With tenant farms came a massive dairy, meat, and wool industry that would help slowly pull New Zealand out of its financial crisis and the creation of roads and towns in the underdeveloped areas that had been ignored since the arrival of the Pākehā. New Zealand became an export-based economy, and Seddon and other Liberal leaders encouraged farmers to export farm products rather than use them to supplement their own diets.

Of course, the improvements made over the 1890s did not only apply to the farmers and rural lands. While the economic situation in the cities gradually improved as the rural lands' exports brought money into the nation, the government wanted to introduce other social security solutions to avoid another devastating financial crisis. In 1898, the Old-age Pension Act was introduced, and restrictions on working hours for women and children came into effect, as did arbitration to settle workplace disputes. While a labor code and workplace insurance were discussed and followed in some workplaces, many business owners ignored the vague workplace rules when they were first introduced. When Richard John Seddon died in 1906, his thirteen-year term ended, making him the longest-serving head of government in New Zealand's history. He was a crude modern leader who greatly contrasted with previous "gentlemanly leaders" who felt worlds away from the people of New Zealand.

Pākehā Identity

Seddon was an avid promoter of nationalist conservatism, as he felt New Zealand's Pākehā identity should be upheld. After the 1880s, most Pākehās living in New Zealand had been born in New Zealand. Yet, despite their birthplace making them New Zealanders, most Pākehā considered themselves British. When New Zealand began exporting farm products, England was its top importer, so much so that New Zealand became known as "Britain's Farmland." When, in 1899, England entered the Second Anglo-Boer War in South Africa, New Zealand supported England by providing troops. In 1901, the New Zealand identity was challenged when Australia became a commonwealth and offered for New Zealand to become one of its states—which New Zealand, of course, turned down.

Māori Affairs at the End of the 19th Century

While Pākehās may have been proudly developing their nation, the original New Zealanders were suffering. By the end of the 19th century, Māori held less than 20 percent of their original land. In every region of

New Zealand where land alienation was studied, it was shown to have generational effects on child mortality, fertility, and the overall health of those affected. While the average life expectancy of a Pākehā girl born in the 1880s was fifty-five, the expected lifespan of a Māori girl was twenty years. Even in the 1890s, 40 percent of Māori girls died before turning one. These stark statistics forced Māori and Pākehās alike to look at the effects of New Zealand's development. Gradually, in the 20th century, Māori health practitioners introduced programs to improve health conditions, fertility, and life expectancies. The New Zealand Pākehā government also aided by introducing social security, better-paying jobs for Māori, and welfare, which would make a massive difference over a few decades. By 1945, the Māori life expectancy had increased from approximately twenty to thirty years to fifty.

Chapter 9 – New Zealand in the 20th Century

The End of the Liberal Era

Seddon would carry New Zealand into the beginning of the 20th century, winning five consecutive elections. During this time, he continued to forge New Zealand's cultural identity and introduce liberal reforms to slowly carry the colony out of its economic depression. After 1901, when New Zealand was encouraged to become a state of Australia, the government focused on solidifying the Pākehā identity. In 1902, New Zealand created its iconic flag, which demonstrated its support of its monarchy through the Union Jack proudly displayed in the corner. Although in 1907 New Zealand would lose its colonial status and become a dominion under the British Empire, it would remain just as connected to the monarchy as it had been as a colony. After Seddon's death in 1906, there were six more years of Liberal government, mostly headlined by Prime Minister Sir Joseph Ward. Ward continued his predecessor's reforms by introducing retirement plans, the National Provident Fund (retirement account), the widows' pensions bill, and other social security measures to avoid devastating economic depressions.

Despite carrying out Seddon's reforms, Ward was certainly not the admired public figure Seddon had been. Ward acted more like a politician, with verbose answers that greatly contrasted with his predecessor's honesty. This lost him the support of the working class, who had been some of Seddon's strongest supporters. By the end of the decade, the people of New Zealand had grown tired of Liberal leaders, none of which could fill the big shoes that Seddon had left in his passing. After convoluted elections, William Ferguson Massey, a dairy farmer, was voted in as prime minister in 1912, heading the newly-created conservative Reform Party (New Zealand Political Reform League).

The Reform Era

William Ferguson Massey, born in Ireland, immigrated to New Zealand to farmland, which earned him his nickname of "Farmer Bill" Massey. Understanding the struggles in pastoral New Zealand, Farmer Bill massively supported the farmers of New Zealand who had become frustrated with the Liberal's tenant farming programs. Prime Minister Massey and the Reform Party had promised that lease-holding farmers would be able to buy the land they had developed at its original value. This promise had little to do with allowing farmers to buy their land, as only a small percentage of New Zealand's farmers were tenants and an even smaller percentage could afford the land they had been lease-holding. The land ownership promise had more to do with ensuring conservative farmers owned their land, that land ownership would not be completely nationalized, and that New Zealand would not become a socialist society.

One complaint many New Zealanders had towards the Liberal Party was that jobs in government were only awarded through favoritism and nepotism. Massey decided to end this political cronyism by creating a Public Service Commissioner, separate from the government, to award public servant jobs. Despite his nickname, Farmer Bill's Cabinet was made up of many businessmen and urban politicians who had earned the jobs through experience rather than comradery, which earned Massey the support of the urban working class. Those who were left-leaning but had lost the support of the Liberal Party eventually formed their own political party, the Labor Party, which would essentially annex the supporters of the Liberal Party.

Discontentment Pre-World War I

Although Massey had the support of the farmers and (mainly wealthy) conservative city folk, the 1910s were marked by general discontent in New Zealand. This dissatisfaction, especially among the lower working class, boiled over in two notable strikes: the 1912 Waihī miners' strike, which would last six disastrous months and end with a fatality, and the

1913 Waterfront Strike and general strikes, which would experience similar violence. The general strike, referred to as the Great Strike of 1913, involved the New Zealand Federation of Labour, created by unionists who disagreed with the Liberal Industrial Conciliation and Arbitration Act of 1894. They felt that workers weren't fairly compensated for their labor and weren't supported by arbiters in workplace disputes. Massey gathered mounted forces to take on the nearly 16,000 unionists who went on strike across the country. Although Massey's forces would manage to defeat the United Federation of Labour, it was not before the strikes halted the entire economy of New Zealand. While conservative farmers continued to support Massey's firm hand, the Reform Party lost the support of those in the cities. According to New Zealand's Russell Museum, after the strike, Massey had the "undying hatred of many urban workers, an enmity passed on to their children."

World War I

As the threat of war in Europe loomed over the 1910s, New Zealand began introducing some military efforts of its own. This began in 1909 with Prime Minister Sir Joseph Ward ordering the construction and financing of a battlecruiser for the United Kingdom's Royal Navy through tens of millions of dollars in taxpayers' money. Although New Zealand was beginning to develop its own sense of nationalism through local associations and sports teams, such as its successful rugby leagues, its economy and culture were still dependent on the success of Britain. Thus, the German threat to the United Kingdom in the early 20th century also threatened the well-being of those in New Zealand.

While serving in the South African War (1899-1902), New Zealanders earned a reputation as strong, superior fighters, which became something the population prided itself on. Thus, it was no surprise when the government of New Zealand introduced the 1909 Defence Act in preparation for the First Great War. The Defence Act forced all able boys between twelve and fourteen to become Junior Cadets and complete fifty-two hours of physical military training. Similar training was made compulsory for older boys. Those ages fourteen to eighteen were required to become Senior Cadets, those eighteen to twenty-one received general training, and those between twenty-one and thirty were conscripted into the reserve. This was, of course, a controversial decision that would spark a massive anti-militarist movement in New Zealand. Still, not all were against the draft, as many viewed it as a way to teach boys necessary discipline, survival skills, morals, and physical health, which had been ignored in schooling.

In August 1914, when England was officially at war, New Zealand was prepared. Thousands of men volunteered to fight, but as the war dragged on, an official draft took place. New Zealand's military made its mark in Gallipoli, Turkey, and France, bringing positive attention to the small nation in the middle of the Pacific Ocean most had barely heard of. While World War I brought many necessary changes to New Zealand, which was still trying to recover from its decades of financial depression, the war was not without its obvious negatives. An estimated 18,500 New Zealanders died defending their monarchy, and 41,000 were wounded. Approximately one out of every three young men from New Zealand (between twenty and forty years old) were wounded or killed in the First World War.

Post-World War I

The effects of the First World War cast a massive shadow on New Zealand's development. That said, the population continued to grow exponentially—so much that in the 1920s, the number of immigrants would more than triple the fighters lost abroad. Over 100,000 immigrants would arrive from England alone, frustrating many New Zealanders, who were forced to share their limited resources with even more people. The birth rate in both Pākehā and Māori societies decreased massively.

In Pākehā society, the smaller, modern nuclear family was becoming the norm, with couples waiting longer to have fewer children than before the war. In Māori society, people were still attempting to fight the diseases and infertility introduced since the widespread European migration to New Zealand. By 1921, there were about four Māori for every 100 Pākehā in New Zealand. After the 1920s, the Māori population grew at the fastest rate since colonization. Post-World War I, Māori mostly lived in pockets of the rural parts of the islands. The Northland and the East Coast became mostly Māori territories, with the Hokianga district and the Bay of Islands having a 64 percent Māori population. As the Māori settled in the country, Pākehās began migrating to urban areas. A third of New Zealand's population was living in the four biggest cities, with Auckland quickly becoming the largest of them all. Californian-style, quick-to-build, affordable suburban homes were becoming the norm, allowing New Zealanders to afford houses despite the urbanization. By 1926, New Zealand had one of the highest rates of home ownership in the world.

The 1920s marked a period of mass development, specifically in farm production, agriculture, electricity, cars, aviation, and railway. Railways and highways were built quickly after the war to help connect the major cities, and by 1930, the number of drivers on the road doubled from 1925. However, despite all the positive technological advancements, the prosperity only lasted a few years after the First World War. By the mid-1920s, New Zealand and the world were beginning to head towards the Great Depression, which would only help to develop massive economic disparities. As New Zealand's economy began to suffer once again, immigration was controversially restricted, especially from Asian countries. The 1920s were almost entirely led by the Reform Party until 1928 when the newly-formed liberal United Party led by Sir Joseph Ward would take their place.

New Zealand Pre-World War II

Just as it had been at the end of the 19th century, New Zealand's economy depended almost entirely on exports. Thus, it would take other foreign countries' economies to bounce back before New Zealand could emerge from its financial depression. Living and working conditions were poor, which led to widespread dissatisfaction and rioting. Despite having recently emerged from the last economic depression, mostly with the help of social security systems in the 1930s, very few programs were introduced to aid the unemployed.

Meanwhile, the newly-formed socialist Labour Party had been gaining popularity, specifically among the working class, who desperately wanted proper welfare programs. However, its strict socialist promises scared off potential voters, leaving them to choose from either the Reform or United parties. In 1931, the United Party's prime minister, George Forbes (who succeeded Ward), decided that he needed help dealing with the Great Depression, which led to the United-Reform coalition government. Although economies overseas had been slowly recovering from the Great Depression by 1934, New Zealand never quite found its way out of its economic hole, leaving most of the population frustrated. Since the main two political parties (which remained in a coalition until 1935) had disappointed the general public, voters were looking for another option to lead their country. The Labour Party, recognizing the need for a new government option in New Zealand, gradually shed its original strong socialist foundation. By focusing less on socialism and more on welfare, tax credits, and guaranteeing farm product prices, the party gained popularity among the increasingly dissatisfied population. Thus, it was no surprise when they succeeded the United-Reform coalition in 1935. Led by Michael Joseph Savage and his successor Peter Fraser, the Labour Party would essentially take control just as prosperity and stability began to return to New Zealand. With its leadership, farmers had safer returns with guaranteed pricing while urban workers had more job options, better working conditions, increased hours, pensions, and higher wages. During the Labour Party's time in office, it strengthened education, medicine, and housing programs and introduced the Social Security Act, which enforced medical and general benefits. After Michael Joseph Savage's four-year stint as prime minister, Peter Fraser was elected in 1940 for a nine-year term, carrying New Zealand through World War II.

World War II

As in World War I, New Zealanders who had earned a reputation and prided themselves on being strong warriors readily joined World War II as soon as Great Britain was involved. However, unlike the previous Great War, New Zealand itself declared war on Germany rather than simply supporting England as a dominion. This time, joining the military was an option for both Pākehā and Māori. Despite it being against the wishes of most Māori elders, approximately 16,000 Māori joined New Zealand's World War II efforts. According to one Māori veteran, the Māori's request to join the war efforts could not be ignored, as their entire upbringing and ancestry had trained them to be warriors.

After once again proving themselves in Europe (specifically in Greece, Italy, and North Africa), many of New Zealand's troops were forced to return when their home was threatened by their nearest axis country: Japan. Although nearly 10 percent of New Zealanders served in the War, New Zealand had a small population, especially compared to their enemy's—New Zealand's population in 1940 made up only 2 percent of Japan's. New Zealand relied on the support of the United States, which ended up dominating the Allied offensive warfare in the Pacific. At home, New Zealand's entire population and economy were focused on the war. Using loans and taxes, the Labour Party managed to keep the economy stabilized and avoid inflation. The effects of World War II were devastating for the world. However, compared to World

War I, New Zealand suffered far less. On a more positive note, like most nations, it would be World War II that helped New Zealand get out of the economic slump it had been trying to fight against since its colonization.

New Zealand Post-World War II
Politics and Foreign Affairs

New Zealand's involvement in World War II helped put the small nation on the international map. During the war, clashes with British military policy encouraged New Zealand's prime minister (Fraser) to demand that New Zealand have a voice on Allied councils separate from that of their monarchy. New Zealand's leader through World War II encouraged the creation of global security and independently signed the United Nations Charter in 1945. After developing a relationship with the United States and other foreign governments during the war, New Zealand began to develop socially and economically to become less dependent on Great Britain. Although Fraser and his successors would begin to seek out their own foreign relations, New Zealand remained a dominion and ally of the United Kingdom.

After the Labour Party took office in 1936, the Liberal and Reform parties decided to officially merge into the National Party. They remained unpopular during the war as they openly opposed the Labour Party's slightly socialist but necessary welfare programs, a stance they eventually let go of. After the nation grew tired of the Labour Party's economic control and rising living prices, the National Party was voted into office in 1949, led by Sidney Holland. Finding creative ways to keep New Zealand's economy alive during a port workers' strike by having the military work the wharves and putting an end to a five-month strike, the National Party gained general favor. Despite a brief period between 1957-1960 when Walter Nash of the Labour Party was voted in as prime minister, the National Party remained in power until 1972, carrying New Zealand into modern times.

After having to be defended by the United States during World War II, new weaknesses revealed to New Zealand fueled post-war foreign affairs. On top of developing relationships with Western powers other than England, New Zealand focused on creating relationships closer to home with other Pacific Islands and Southeast Asian countries. In 1949, New Zealand helped the British fight in Malaya, and the following year,

New Zealand joined the UN's British Commonwealth force in Korea. Despite its small population, New Zealand participated in many wars that threatened global security. For example, in 1954, it aided its new ally, the United States, in Vietnam. Most of New Zealand's warring in post-World War II seemed to be founded on the fear of communism in nearby Asian countries. Of course, not all New Zealanders were on board. As New Zealand's military hopped from one communist war to another, anti-war protests grew in popularity until, finally, in the 1970s, the nation's military pulled out of Vietnam altogether.

Economy

Despite forming new foreign relationships, after the war, New Zealand's economy was still mostly dependent on being "Britain's farmyard," just as before. It is estimated that about half of New Zealand's exports in the 1950s went to the United Kingdom, and 90 percent of all exports were farm products—specifically meat, wool, and dairy. Even by the end of the 1960s, when exportations diversified a bit, more than a third of New Zealand's exports were still going to the United Kingdom. Of course, an economy entirely dependent on agriculture and Britain's demand could not remain stable. This became obvious towards the end of the 1950s when wool and butter prices dropped, severely affecting New Zealand's economy. In the 1960s when a similar drop occurred in wool prices and England began importing from nearer European countries, New Zealand entered an economic recession. By 1976, after oil prices skyrocketed and exports to England dropped to less than 15 percent, New Zealand was in an economic crisis. As mentioned, the National Party remained in power until 1972, when the economic recession left New Zealanders searching for new leadership that could offer better social security. The popular Labour Party leader Norman Kirk was voted in as prime minister, a position he would keep for less than two years before passing away. He was succeeded by two Labour Party leaders, who would hold the government until 1975.

Population and Culture

Like other nations, New Zealand experienced a baby boom and increased immigration post-World War II. During the decade after the war, around 400,000 babies were born, and over 125,000 immigrants settled in New Zealand, ultimately bumping the population to approximately 2.3 million people by 1959. This number continued to grow exponentially, and in 1961 alone, over 60,000 babies were born in

New Zealand. Births and immigration would continue to skyrocket until the economic recession and introduction of the birth control pill towards the end of the 1960s. The population also decreased due to emigration, with many New Zealanders choosing to move to Australia and other larger countries with more business opportunities. By the end of the 1970s, the population of New Zealand reached around 3.2 million people, with most of the growth concentrated in the first fifteen years after the war.

Of course, with the rising Pākehā population, Māori New Zealanders suffered. In the years after World War II, Māori still had a life expectancy nearly twenty years less than that of Pākehā New Zealanders, mostly due to the high infant death rates in Māori communities. A large reason for this was the lack of medical services in the impoverished rural communities Māori were forced into. By the 1970s, the gap between the life expectancies of Pākehā and Māori decreased to only seven years, largely thanks to the second mass Māori migration, in which most Māori left the country to live in the cities. By 1971, nearly three-quarters of Māori were living in urban areas, mostly due to their involvement in the war, which helped integrate them into Pākehā society and give them social security. The Māori migration to the cities was also due to the demand for workers in manufacturing jobs, which Pākehā were leaving in exchange for higher-paying jobs. By 1970, the rate of child mortality had halved, and by 1976, Māori had built up a young population, with almost half under the age of sixteen.

After the World Wars, New Zealand continued developing its distinct culture, often summed up by "rugby, racing, and beer." Although rugby had been popular before the war, it became a massive cultural phenomenon. Cricket and motor racing attracted fans as well. During World War I, New Zealand had introduced the "Six o'clock swill" where patrons of pubs would consume as much beer as possible before the 6 p.m. closing time. This measure, which allowed New Zealanders to avoid prohibition, remained in place into the 1960s, training generations of Kiwis to quickly consume mass amounts of alcohol before the evening.

Otherwise, the 1960s began decades of protests in New Zealand. From environmental issues and anti-military movements to union and feminist riots, post-war New Zealanders were focused on reforms. As before the wars, social security and labor reforms were slowly introduced throughout the 20th century. However, something that changed at a far faster pace was women's rights. By the late 1970s, New Zealand had women in higher positions of government than most nations in the world.

New Zealand at the End of the 20th Century

Politics and Economy

In the years after the Second World War, New Zealand had become a wealthy nation with a high standard of living. By 1965, it was the sixth wealthiest country per capita. However, by the late 1970s, New Zealand's economic standing had fallen, and it ranked as the 19th wealthiest country per capita. In 1975, Sir Robert Muldoon of the National Party was voted in as prime minister, a position he would keep until 1984. During his almost nine-year tenure in office, he tried to combat the economic recession that had once again befallen on New Zealand in the form of unemployment and inflation. In 1982, Muldoon froze the nation's wages and prices, which helped combat inflation but did little to help New Zealand's economy. To oppose unemployment, Muldoon financed industrial developments that New Zealand did not have the budget for, requiring the government to go into debt, borrowing funds from other countries.

As the population grew dissatisfied with the National government's failed attempts at intervention, an election was held in 1984, and David Lange of the Labour Party was voted in as prime minister. Part of Lange's popularity came from his party's anti-nuclear weapon stance, which affected relations with the United States. David Lange and his two Labour Party successors, known as the Fourth Labour Government, focused on reversing almost all the economic policies and restriction enacted before World War II. Some examples of these changes include the lowering of income taxes, the restructuring and corporatizing of government departments, and the elimination of agricultural subsidies. On top of these massive reforms, Lange lifted all controls on interest rates, foreign conversion rates, product prices, and wages. These free-market reforms, which were not all popular among a population unused to this much change, were dubbed "Rogernomics," named after the Minister of Finance Roger Douglas.

Although these measures helped to improve inflation rates by the late 1980s, unemployment was still high due to the removal of subsidies, which caused many farmers to lose their farms, as well as the privatization of government enterprises, which meant those working in public service no longer had job security. In 1988, Lange felt Douglas was taking his economic reforms too far and was let go, specifically because of his push for a flat tax rate. However, Douglas was controversial, and ultimately this decision hurt the Labour Party since he had many supporters who felt he was New Zealand's only hope for fixing its economy. Roger Douglas was brought back into the Labour Party's Cabinet by 1989. With Douglas' return, Lange felt it was time to step down as prime minister. He was briefly replaced by two short-lived Labour Party leaders before the general election in 1990 when the National Party, led by Jim Bolger, retook the government by a landslide vote.

Overall, many of the economic reforms Roger Douglas and David Lange introduced benefited the wealthy but hurt the poor. One example of this was the 1986 tax on goods and services, which allowed the highest earners in New Zealand's tax rate to drop by over 20 percent. Māori were also affected by Rogernomics. The corporatizing of government departments left many of those who depended on government industries jobless, and the Māori unemployment rate rose 15 percent higher than that of the Pākehā.

Under the National Party, Bolger remained anti-nuclear weapons, helped fight unemployment, and repaired the economy. However, by the end of the 20th century, most New Zealanders were disillusioned with both the National and Labour parties. Under the FPP (first-past-the-post) voting system, which forced voters to choose one electoral candidate to represent them, it was unlikely for there to be more than two political parties to choose from. Despite third political parties often getting 20 percent of the votes, voters knew it was not worth voting for a party other than Labour or National, as it was a two-party race. In the 1980s, a Royal Commission was created to discuss the adoption of a new voting system, the MMP (mixed member proportional), inspired by the one in Germany.

After a series of referendums, New Zealand introduced its new voting system in 1996, just as Jim Bolger resigned. There would be 120 Parliament seats available, and voters would be not only electing a prime minister but also who represented the nation in Parliament. Under New Zealand's MMP system, voters voted twice—once for their party of choice, which decided who would be prime minister and how many seats each party received at Parliament, and once for who would represent their area in Parliament, known as electorate MPs. Since, under the new MMP system, parties rarely had the majority of the seats in at Parliament anymore, agreements and coalitions among MPs and parties became necessary. This occurred in the 1996 election, in which the National Party formed a coalition with the much smaller New Zealand First Party. With the previous leader having stepped down, the National Party had the chance to elect its own leader, finally deciding on New Zealand's first female prime minister, Jennifer Shipley.

By the end of the 1990s, the faults in the MMP system were revealed as the coalition between the National Party and the New Zealand First Party fell apart, leaving Jennifer Shipley with a minority government that struggled to make necessary changes. As New Zealand once again headed towards a financial crisis at the end of the 20th century, the National Party, without a majority, lost public favor as few social security measures were introduced.

Population and Culture

By the end of the 20th century, New Zealand had a population of around 3.8 million, with two-thirds of that population living on North Island. Around half of the population lived (and still lives) in the three biggest cities: Auckland and Wellington on North Island and Christchurch on South Island. Auckland grew to be the biggest city in New Zealand, with nearly one-quarter of the population. By the end of the 20th century, the Māori's previously shrinking population had begun to grow again. Still, the European population outnumbered the Māori in New Zealand by approximately eight times. By the end of the 20th century, Māori issues started to be taken more seriously by New Zealand's population, which became obvious with the boycott of Waitangi Day throughout the 1980s.

By the 1980s, the first popular local Kiwi and Māori television shows were being made, although shows from England and the United States still dominated New Zealand's TV screens. A similar pattern occurred with music, movies, and books, with the 1980s spearheading the popularity of Pākehā and Māori-made art. Sports remained the most popular pastime for most New Zealanders. However, a dark shadow was cast on rugby, specifically after a rugby tour in the 1980s in South Africa led to some of New Zealand's most violent protests.

By the end of the 20th century, many technological advancements had become widespread in New Zealand, including personal vehicles, televisions, mobile phones, and microwaves. Meanwhile, as technology modernized, the population did as well, as seen in the change in women's employment rates. In 1961, one sixth of married women were working full- time. By 1981, that doubled to one third. By 2000, most women were working, making up 45 percent of New Zealand's workforce. This transition occurred much faster in New Zealand than in most countries, demonstrating the speed of the nation's modernization.

Chapter 10 – New Zealand Today (2000–Present)

Helen Clark 1999-2008

After the National and New Zealand First Party coalition began to fall apart due to internal factionalism, the population grew tired of the government. Dissatisfaction with the National Party's 1990s politics grew exponentially after it introduced reforms to the retirement superannuation savings system. By the end of the 19th century, New Zealand wanted a change. So, during the 1999 election, Helen Clark of the Labour Party, which had formed a coalition with the Alliance Party, was voted in as the first women prime minister elected by the people. Through a variety of coalitions with smaller parties, Helen Clark's Labour Party would remain in government for nearly nine years, during which it would help New Zealand catch up with policies around the world. A minimum wage, voluntary retirement savings accounts, and family income support were introduced. Overall, the economy and society prospered under the Fifth Labour Government until 2006, when inflation rates and unemployment began rising just before the 2008 financial crisis.

During the early 2000s, there were many debates and protests regarding Māori affairs. In 2004, a massive controversy broke out related to the attempted nationalization of New Zealand's foreshore and seabed. Many Māori believed the century-and-a-half-old Treaty of Waitangi gave them a rightful claim to their ancestral land on the island's oceanfront.

Despite many large protests, in November, the government passed the Foreshore and Seabed Act 2004, which nationalized New Zealand's beaches. Still, it continued allowing Māori the right to fish and gather on their ancestral lands. After generations of mistreatment, Māori frustration had reached an all-time high in the 21st century, especially after further land seizures (like that of the beaches), which many New Zealanders feared would result in Māori terrorism. This Pākehā fear culminated in the 2007 New Zealand police raids, in which hundreds of armed police violently broke into the homes of a Māori village in the Urewera mountain range, seizing computers, files, and weapons. While the jury could not agree whether the Māori involved had an organized terrorist criminal group, eighteen Māori were arrested and charged with owning firearms. After many similar issues and years of protests, many ancestors of New Zealand's first people found themselves frustrated with their government, which resulted in nearly a sixth of the Māori population relocating to Australia. Even today, Brisbane, Australia, has the second-highest population of Māori, only behind Auckland. Māori remaining in New Zealand would continue to fight for Māori rights and the use of the Māori te reo language in schools, news, and all government offices.

John Key 2008-2016

By the end of the early 2000s, the 2008 economic crisis had hit New Zealand, and once again, the population became frustrated with the government they viewed as overprotective. This dissatisfaction resulted in John Key and the National Party being voted in during the 2008 elections in coalition with the Māori Party and other smaller parties. Key became prime minister at a poor time, as New Zealand sank further into its longest recession in history, yet he remained focused on economic reforms. Key referred to his government's policies as "the largest economic undertaking in New Zealand's history." By 2013, his work proved successful, as New Zealand was one of the first nations to emerge from the recession. Key remained New Zealand's leader for eight years until his resignation. A fellow National Party leader, Bill English, held the position for a little less than a year. During their government, New Zealand suffered through not only the economic crisis but a series of earthquakes—the most notable, fatal, and destructive in Christchurch in 2011. Despite his inherited roadblocks, John Key remained extremely popular, especially with his modern reforms, such as the legalization of same-sex marriage in 2013. Under the National government, Māori also enjoyed advancements, the most notable of which was the 2017 Whanganui River bill, which recognized the river as having the same rights as a living entity—the same rights as humans. This was a big win for the Māori, who no longer have to fear the seizure of the river they view as integral to their community's survival.

Jacinda Ardern 2017–2023

After a series of inconclusive elections in 2017 that demonstrated the complications that could arise from the MPP voting system, the new thirty-seven-year-old Labour Party leader Jacinda Ardern attempted to form a coalition government. Though the Green Party announced it would support Ardern's Labour Party through confidence and supply, this would not be enough to form a majority, as together they only held forty-five and seven seats, respectively. This was less than Bill English's National Party, which held fifty-eight seats in Parliament, but also not enough for a majority. It would be up to the New Zealand First Party, holding nine seats, to decide between the National and Labour. However, Winston Peters, the New Zealand First leader, decided not to form a coalition with either until all votes, including overseas special votes, were tallied. This put the nation in quite a limbo awaiting voting results. After many negotiations, Peters decided to back the Labour Party, helping elect one of the world's youngest leaders as prime minister. The following year, Ardern would have her first child while in office.

Ardern and the Labour Party would continue to lead New Zealand for just over five years, during which the nation and the world would undergo some very intense disasters and transformations. One of the more horrific events in New Zealand's history, which gained worldwide attention, was the 2018 Christchurch mosque shootings. One Australian white supremacist live-streamed his murder of fifty-one people and injury of fifty more. This event occurred after the man posted an over seventy-page manifesto laying out his hatred for immigrants and his plans for the attack. Although police managed to apprehend the terrorist before he used the explosive devices he had prepared, it was far too late. In 2019, New Zealand suffered another loss, this time from nature, when a volcanic eruption on White Island (Whakaari) killed twenty-one tourists and guides. The country got little time to relax as, at the beginning of 2020, the world was hit by the coronavirus pandemic, which

Ardern decided to tackle quickly by instantly shutting down New Zealand from internal travel and external visitors. Overall, New Zealand would have one of the more successful strategies for handling the pandemic and was able to reopen before most other countries (despite subsequent lockdowns). Of course, the strict policies, especially related to vaccination mandates, were unpopular among many. In 2022, a freedom convoy threatening Ardern's life stormed Parliament. Law enforcement arrested protestors, but by this time, Ardern had had enough, resigning as prime minister in January of 2023. The Labour Party decided to replace Ardern with New Zealand's forty-four-year-old health minister, Chris Hipkins, who had experience in government handling the nation's response to the pandemic.

Conclusion

Today, New Zealand is known for being an incredibly beautiful country near Australia, this reputation likely due to its landscapes being the filming location of *The Lord of the Rings* franchise. While Australia is New Zealand's nearest neighbor, the two islands in the Pacific Ocean have their own culturally-rich, complex histories that greatly differ.

After its delayed settlement and colonization, New Zealand developed exponentially. Despite slow economic and population growth, it modernized politically and culturally faster than most other countries. Perhaps the smaller population allowed New Zealand's government to focus on reforms.

But, whatever the reason, New Zealand has always been ahead of its time, even in its treatment of the indigenous Māori population. While the Māori did suffer due to European settlement, the indigenous people of New Zealand were extremely immersed in political affairs and remained culturally strong in comparison to natives in other colonized lands. Despite having had less time to develop than most countries and its various natural disasters and economic setbacks, New Zealand has become a global powerhouse known for military involvement and exportations.

Today, the remote islands of New Zealand still have a small population, but that population of only five million is culturally diverse. Approximately 15 percent of New Zealand is of Māori descent, 60 percent is of various European descent, and 12 percent is of Asian descent. Of the entire population, an estimated one quarter is born elsewhere, demonstrating the lure that these small, remote islands in the Pacific have to those abroad.

Here's another book by Captivating History that you might like

Free Bonus from Captivating History (Available for a Limited time)

Hi History Lovers!

Now you have a chance to join our exclusive history list so you can get your first history ebook for free as well as discounts and a potential to get more history books for free! Simply visit the link below to join.

Captivatinghistory.com/ebook

Also, make sure to follow us on Facebook, Twitter and Youtube by searching for Captivating History.

Bibliography

Alves, T. (2018, June 28). The story of colonisation in New Zealand. Retrieved March, 2023, from https://theculturetrip.com/pacific/new-zealand/articles/the-story-of-colonisation-in-new-zealand/

Angas, G., & New Zealand Ministry for Culture and Heritage Te Manatu Taonga. (2010, March 11). Pātaka. Retrieved March, 2023, from https://teara.govt.nz/en/artwork/23447/pataka

Aspin, C. (2019, January 22). Early Māori sexuality. Retrieved March, 2023, from https://teara.govt.nz/en/hokakatanga-maori-sexualities/page-2

BBC. (2017, March 15). New Zealand River first in the world to be given legal human status. Retrieved March, 2023, from https://www.bbc.com/news/world-asia-39282918

BBC. (2022, October 10). New Zealand profile - timeline. Retrieved March, 2023, from https://www.bbc.com/news/world-asia-pacific-15370160

Biggs, B. (1970). Māori marriage: An essay in reconstruction. Wellington: A.H. & A.W. Reed.

Blyth, Conrad Alexander, Dalziel, Raewyn, Oliver, William Hosking, Sinclair, Keith, Moran, Warren and Vowles, Jack. (2022, December). New Zealand. Retrieved March, 2023, from https://www.britannica.com/place/New-Zealand

Boissoneault, L. (2018, August 24). Captain Cook's 1768 voyage to the South Pacific included a secret mission. Retrieved March, 2023, from https://www.smithsonianmag.com/history/captain-cooks-1768-voyage-south-pacific-included-secret-mission-180970119/

Britannica, The Editors of Encyclopedia. (2014, September 1). New Zealand Company. Retrieved March, 2023, from https://www.britannica.com/topic/New-Zealand-Company

Britannica, The Editors of Encyclopedia. (2022, August 26). Māori. Retrieved March, 2023, from https://www.britannica.com/topic/Maori

Britannica, The Editors of Encyclopedia. (2022, November). William Ferguson Massey. Retrieved March, 2023, from https://www.britannica.com/biography/William-Ferguson-Massey

Britannica, The Editors of Encyclopedia. (2023, February 22). Māori language. Retrieved March, 2023, from https://www.britannica.com/topic/Maori-language

The British Museum. (2021, February 26). Porcelain, gold, and the Dutch East India Company. Retrieved March, 2023, from https://smarthistory.org/porcelain-gold-dutch-east-india-company/

Brown, A. A., & Crema, E. R. (2019, May 21). Māori population growth in pre-contact New Zealand: Regional population dynamics inferred from summed probability distributions of radiocarbon dates. Retrieved March, 2023, from https://www.tandfonline.com/doi/full/10.1080/15564894.2019.1605429

Colin James. (2021, September 24). National Party. Retrieved March, 2023, from https://teara.govt.nz/en/national-party

Cook, J. (1824). The journals of captain James Cook on his voyages of Discovery. London: Hakluyt Society.

Cook, M. (2017, May 1). Marriage in traditional Māori Society. Retrieved March, 2023, from https://teara.govt.nz/en/marriage-and-partnering/page-1#1

Corlett, E. (2022, August 10). Aotearoa or New Zealand: Has the moment come to change the country's name? Retrieved March, 2023, from https://www.theguardian.com/world/2022/aug/11/aotearoa-or-new-zealand-has-the-moment-come-to-change-the-countrys-name

Dongen, Y. V. (1992, July–September). The Invisible Immigrants. New Zealand Geographic, (015).

Doucleff, M. (2013, January 23). How the sweet potato crossed the pacific way before the Europeans did. Retrieved March, 2023, from https://www.npr.org/sections/thesalt/2013/01/22/169980441/how-the-sweet-potato-crossed-the-pacific-before-columbus

Dunmore, J. (2021, September 07). Marion du Fresne, Marc Joseph. Retrieved March, 2023, from https://teara.govt.nz/en/biographies/1m13/marion-du-fresne-marc-joseph

Electoral Commission New Zealand. (2021). What is MMP? Retrieved March, 2023, from https://elections.nz/democracy-in-nz/what-is-new-zealands-system-of-government/what-is-mmp/

Enviro History New Zealand. (2010, June 7). Māori gardening in pre-European NZ. Retrieved March, 2023, from https://envirohistorynz.com/2010/06/07/maori-gardening-in-pre-european-nz/

Evans, K. (2018, November/December). Return of the Lost Birds. New Zealand Geographic, (154).

Fairfax Media Australia. (2004, November 19). NZ passes law to nationalise coast. The Sydney Morning Herald.

Georg Forster. (1772).

Griffin, M., Dr. (2022). Continuing the voyages of the endeavour. Retrieved March, 2023, from https://royalsociety.org/science-events-and-lectures/2006/endeavour/

Haerewa, N. (2020, March 18). Māori culture: What is a marae? Retrieved March, 2023, from https://theculturetrip.com/pacific/new-zealand/articles/maori-culture-what-is-a-marae/Hawke, E., Brett, P., & Spencer, C. (1768, July 30). Additional Instructions for Lt James Cook, Appointed to Command His Majesty's Bark the Endeavour.

Hearn, T. (2012, November 15). "New Zealand wants domestic servants." Retrieved March, 2023, from https://teara.govt.nz/en/ephemera/1901/new-zealand-wants-domestic-servants

Higgins, R. (2013, September 5). Origins of TĀ moko. Retrieved March, 2023, from https://teara.govt.nz/en/ta-moko-maori-tattooing/page-1

Hobson, J. (2019, July 08). 250 years ago, captain Cook embarked on first of three voyages. Retrieved March, 2023, from https://www.wbur.org/hereandnow/2019/07/08/captain-james-cook-legacy

Hollingsworth, J. (2020, December 12). This river in New Zealand is legally a person. here's how it happened. Retrieved March, 2023, from https://www.cnn.com/2020/12/11/asia/whanganui-river-new-zealand-intl-hnk-dst/index.html

Hunter, Michael. (2021, January 24). Royal Society. Retrieved March, 2023, from https://www.britannica.com/topic/Royal-Society

IStudent Complaints. (2020, September 3). Seven kiwi animals that went extinct and two that came back for international students to know. Retrieved March, 2023, from https://www.istudent.org.nz/resources/seven-kiwi-animals-went-extinct-and-two-came-back-international-students-know

K. A. Simpson. (2020, August 24). Hobson, William. Retrieved March, 2023, from https://teara.govt.nz/en/biographies/1h29/hobson-william

KDSMurray. (2009, February 08). Dumont D'Urville's Epic Tale of the Noble New Zealander. Retrieved March, 2023, from http://ideaofsouth.net/region/pacific/dumont-durvilles-epic-tale-of-the-noble-new-zealander

Keane, B. (2011, May 5). Ngā Atua – the gods. Retrieved March, 2023, from https://teara.govt.nz/en/traditional-maori-religion-nga-karakia-a-te-maori/page-1

Keane, B. (2021, October 28). Musket wars. Retrieved March, 2023, from https://teara.govt.nz/en/musket-wars

Keenan, D. (2017, October 14). "Anti-terror" raids failed to find a smoking gun. New Zealand Herald Whanganui Chronicle.

Kästle, K. (2023). New Zealand. Retrieved March, 2023, from https://www.nationsonline.org/oneworld/new_zealand.htm

Lange, R. (2021, October 06). Te Hauora Māori i mua – history of Māori health. Retrieved March, 2023, from https://teara.govt.nz/en/te-hauora-maori-i-mua-history-of-maori-health

Lindauer, G., & Royal, T. (2007, September 24). "Tohunga under tapu." Retrieved March, 2023, from https://teara.govt.nz/en/artwork/7967/tohunga-under-tapu

Lock, A. (2013, November 7). On this day: Mungo Man Fossil found. Retrieved March, 2023, from https://www.australiangeographic.com.au/blogs/on-this-day/2013/11/on-this-day-mungo-man-fossil-found/

Love, M., & Love, T. (2010, March 11). History of Māori enterprise. Retrieved March, 2023, from https://teara.govt.nz/en/nga-umanga-maori-business-enterprise/page-1

Mackay, D. (2007, November). Cook, James. Retrieved March, 2023, from https://teara.govt.nz/en/biographies/1c25/cook-james

Mansfield, L. (2021, September 16). New Zealand: Prehistoric giant penguin species identified from fossil found by schoolchildren. Retrieved March, 2023, from https://news.sky.com/story/new-zealand-prehistoric-giant-penguin-species-identified-from-fossil-found-by-schoolchildren-12409671

Māori Source. (2023). The Māori people. Retrieved March, 2023, from http://maorisource.com/Maori.html

Marlborough District Council. (2023). Allports Island. Retrieved March, 2023, from https://cruiseguide.co.nz/queen-charlotte-sound/allports-island

McLintock, A., & R.f. (2009, April 22). Traditional social structure. Retrieved March, 2023, from https://teara.govt.nz/en/1966/maori-social-structure/page-2

McLintock, A., & Sharp, C. (2009, April 22). Naming of New Zealand. Retrieved March, 2023, from https://teara.govt.nz/en/1966/new-zealand-naming-of/page-2

McLintock, A., Cyril Roy Knight, M., & New Zealand Ministry for Culture and Heritage Te Manatu Taonga. (2009, April 22). Conclusion. Retrieved March, 2023, from https://teara.govt.nz/en/1966/towns-and-cities-growth-of/page-8

McLintock, A., Jock Malcolm McEwen, L., & New Zealand Ministry for Culture and Heritage Te Manatu Taonga. (2009, April 22). Intertribal conflicts. Retrieved March, 2023, from https://teara.govt.nz/en/1966/maori-tribal-history

McLintock, A., John Victor Tuwhakahewa Baker, M., & New Zealand Ministry for Culture and Heritage Te Manatu Taonga. (2009, April 22). Population, population trends, and the census. Retrieved March, 2023, from https://teara.govt.nz/en/1966/population

McMillan, Neale. (2022, August 5). John Key. Retrieved March, 2023, from https://www.britannica.com/biography/John-Key

McSaveney, E., & Nathan, S. (2006, June 12). Geology – overview. Retrieved March, 2023, from https://teara.govt.nz/en/geology-overview

Meijer, H. (2016, August 24). How did the chicken, a shy, flight-impaired forest bird, migrate around the globe? Retrieved March, 2023, from https://www.theguardian.com/science/2016/aug/24/how-did-the-chicken-a-shy-forest-bird-migrate-around-the-globe-new-zealan

Ministry for Culture and Heritage. (2006, June 12). First Sitting, 1854. Retrieved March, 2023, from https://nzhistory.govt.nz/politics/history-of-parliament/first-sitting-1854

Ministry for Culture and Heritage. (2014, August 5). New Zealand and the Second World War. Retrieved March, 2023, from https://nzhistory.govt.nz/war/new-zealand-and-the-second-world-war-overview

Ministry for Culture and Heritage. (2014, August 5). New Zealand and the United Nations. Retrieved March, 2023, from https://nzhistory.govt.nz/politics/new-zealand-and-the-united-nations

Ministry for Culture and Heritage. (2016, April 4). United Tribes Flag. Retrieved March, 2023, from https://nzhistory.govt.nz/culture/taming-the-frontier/united-tribes-flag

Ministry for Culture and Heritage. (2016, January 13). First past the Post. Retrieved March, 2023, from https://nzhistory.govt.nz/politics/fpp-to-mmp/first-past-the-post

Ministry for Culture and Heritage. (2017, August 18). The Northern War. Retrieved March, 2023, from https://nzhistory.govt.nz/war/northern-war

Ministry for Culture and Heritage. (2017, November 8). George Grey. Retrieved March, 2023, from https://nzhistory.govt.nz/people/sir-george-grey

Ministry for Culture and Heritage. (2018, April 30). The 1920s. Retrieved March, 2023, from https://nzhistory.govt.nz/culture/the-1920s

Ministry for Culture and Heritage. (2018, May 1). The 1950s. Retrieved March, 2023, from https://nzhistory.govt.nz/culture/the-1950s/overview

Ministry for Culture and Heritage. (2018, May 9). The 1960s. Retrieved March, 2023, from https://nzhistory.govt.nz/culture/the-1960s/overview

Ministry for Culture and Heritage. (2018, September 24). Māori King movement origins. Retrieved March, 2023, from https://nzhistory.govt.nz/politics/the-maori-king-movement/te-kingitanga/introduction

Ministry for Culture and Heritage. (2019, April 9). Thomas Gore Browne. Retrieved March, 2023, from https://nzhistory.govt.nz/people/thomas-browne

Ministry for Culture and Heritage. (2020, February 4). The 1981 Springbok Rugby Tour. Retrieved March, 2023, from https://nzhistory.govt.nz/culture/1981-springbok-tour

Ministry for Culture and Heritage. (2020, July 13). History of New Zealand, 1769-1914. Retrieved March, 2023, from https://nzhistory.govt.nz/culture/history-of-new-zealand-1769-1914

Ministry for Culture and Heritage. (2020, May 1). Māori and the Second World War. Retrieved March, 2023, from https://nzhistory.govt.nz/war/maori-in-second-world-war

Ministry for Culture and Heritage. (2020, November 5). "King Dick" Seddon becomes premier. Retrieved March, 2023, from https://nzhistory.govt.nz/richard-seddon-becomes-premier

Ministry for Culture and Heritage. (2020, October 5). D'Urville sails through "French pass." Retrieved March, 2023, from https://nzhistory.govt.nz/durville-sails-through-french-pass

Ministry for Culture and Heritage. (2020, September 15). Coalition government formed to combat depression. Retrieved March, 2023, from https://nzhistory.govt.nz/honest-george-forbes-establishes-a-united-reform-coalition-government-to-combat-the-depression

Ministry for Culture and Heritage. (2020, September 18). "Six o'clock swill" begins. Retrieved March, 2023, from https://nzhistory.govt.nz/the-six-oclock-swill-begins

Ministry for Culture and Heritage. (2020, September 24). New Zealand constitution act comes into force. Retrieved March, 2023, from https://nzhistory.govt.nz/proclamation-of-1852-constitution-act

Ministry for Culture and Heritage. (2021, October 20). The Wairau Incident. Retrieved March, 2023, from https://nzhistory.govt.nz/war/wairau-incident

Ministry for Culture and Heritage. (2021, October 4). Māori and European population numbers, 1838–1901. Retrieved March, 2023, from https://nzhistory.govt.nz/media/photo/maori-and-european-population-numbers-1838%E2%80%931901

Ministry for Culture and Heritage. (2021, October 4). The 1980s. Retrieved March, 2023, from https://nzhistory.govt.nz/culture/the-1980s/overview

Ministry for Culture and Heritage. (2021, September 28). The 1970s. Retrieved March, 2023, from https://nzhistory.govt.nz/culture/the-1970s/overview

Ministry for Culture and Heritage. (2022, January 13). He Whakaputanga - Declaration of Independence. Retrieved March, 2023, from https://nzhistory.govt.nz/culture/declaration-of-independence-taming-the-frontier

Ministry of Business Innovation and Employment. (2023). Tapu and noa. Retrieved March, 2023, from https://www.iponz.govt.nz/about-ip/maori-ip/concepts-to-understand/

The Minnesota Governor's Council on Developmental Disabilities. (2023). Parallels in time: A history of developmental disabilities. Retrieved March, 2023, from https://mn.gov/mnddc/parallels/three/2.html

National Army Museum Te Mata Toa. (2022, August 12). Māori weapons. Retrieved March, 2023, from https://www.armymuseum.co.nz/maori-weapons/

The National Library of Australia. (2023). Who was the first European to land on "terra australis"? Retrieved March, 2023, from https://www.nla.gov.au/faq/who-was-the-first-european-to-land-on-australia

National Library of New Zealand. (2023). Te Kauri, active 1772. Retrieved March, 2023, from https://natlib.govt.nz/records/22471198

National Museum of Australia Press. (2010). Exploration and Endeavour: The Royal Society of London and the South Seas.

New Zealand Geographic. (2023). Prehistoric Aotearoa. Retrieved March, 2023, from https://www.nzgeo.com/prehistoric/

New Zealand Immigration. (2022, July 14). A brief history. Retrieved March, 2023, from https://www.live-work.immigration.govt.nz/live-in-new-zealand/history-government/a-brief-history

New Zealand Parliament. (2020, March 3). The history of New Zealand's Party System. Retrieved March, 2023, from https://www.parliament.nz/mi/get-involved/features/the-history-of-new-zealands-party-system/

New Zealand Tourism. (2023). Captain Cook's Landing Site and Young Nick's Head. Retrieved March, 2023, from https://www.newzealand.com/ca/feature/captain-cooks-landing-site-and-young-nicks-head/

New Zealand Tourism. (2023). Marae: Māori meeting ground. Retrieved March, 2023, from https://www.newzealand.com/au/feature/marae-maori-meeting-grounds/

New Zealand Tourism. (2023). Pōwhiri: Welcome Ceremony. Retrieved March, 2023, from https://www.newzealand.com/ca/feature/powhiri-maori-welcome/

New Zealand Tourism. (2023). Raranga: Māori weaving. Retrieved March, 2023, from https://www.newzealand.com/int/maori-weaving/

New Zealand Tourism. (2023). The Arrival of Europeans: New Zealand. Retrieved March, 2023, from https://www.newzealand.com/int/feature/europeans-arrive-to-aotearoa/

New Zealand Tourism. (2023). Toi: Māori art. Retrieved March, 2023, from https://www.newzealand.com/ca/feature/maori-arts/

Newnham, R. M., Lowe, D. J., McGlone, M. S., Wilmshurst, J. M., & Higham, T. F. (2002, May 25). The Kaharoa tephra as a critical datum for earliest human impact in northern New Zealand. Retrieved March, 2023, from https://www.sciencedirect.com/science/article/abs/pii/S030544039790217X

Oliver, S. (2020, July 29). Maketū, Wiremu Kīngi. Retrieved March, 2023, from https://teara.govt.nz/en/biographies/1m5/maketu-wiremu-kingi

O'Malley, V. (Writer). (2015, May 26). 18th Century Māori travellers [Radio series episode]. In Nine To Noon. Radio New Zealand.

O'Neill, A. (2022, June 21). Population of New Zealand 1820-2020. Retrieved March, 2023, from https://www.statista.com/statistics/1066999/population-new-zealand-historical/

Pool, I., & Kukutai, T. (2018). Retrieved from https://teara.govt.nz/en/taupori-maori-maori-population-change/page-2

Orange, C. (2020, July 31). Busby, James. Retrieved March, 2023, from https://teara.govt.nz/en/biographies/1b54/busby-james

Orange, C. (2021, July 08). Treaty of Waitangi. Retrieved March, 2023, from https://teara.govt.nz/en/treaty-of-waitangi

Princeton University Library. (2010). Abel Janszoon Tasman. Retrieved March, 2023, from https://library.princeton.edu/visual_materials/maps/websites/pacific/tasman/tasman.html

Pskhun. (2022, March 10). Miotadorna catrionae A New Species of Large Duck. Retrieved March, 2023, from http://novataxa.blogspot.com/2022/03/miotadorna.html

R. L. Weitzel. (1973). Pacifists and Anti-militarists in New Zealand, 1909–1914. New Zealand Journal of History, 7(2), 128-147.

Rawlence, N. (2022, June 16). New Zealand should celebrate its remarkable prehistoric past with national fossil emblems – have your say! Retrieved March, 2023, from https://theconversation.com/new-zealand-should-celebrate-its-remarkable-prehistoric-past-with-national-fossil-emblems-have-your-say-184942

Rousseau, J.J. (1895). Social Contract. London: Swan Sonnenschein & Co.

Royal Society of New Zealand Te Apārangi. (2023). Joan Wiffen. Retrieved March, 2023, from https://www.royalsociety.org.nz/150th-anniversary/150-women-in-150-words/1968-2017/joan-wiffen/

Royal, C., & Kaka-Scott, J. (2013, September 5). Māori foods - Kai Māori. Retrieved March, 2023, from https://teara.govt.nz/en/maori-foods-kai-maori

Russell Museum. (2016, February 7). Electioneering 100 years ago? Retrieved March, 2023, from https://www.russellmuseum.org.nz/electioneering-100-years-ago-165/

Salmond, A. (2016). Aphrodite's Island: The European discovery of Tahiti. North Shore, N.Z.: Penguin/Viking.

Simpson, M. J. (2021, September 07). Dumont d'Urville, Jules Sébastien César. Retrieved March, 2023, from https://teara.govt.nz/en/biographies/1d19/dumont-durville-jules-sebastien-cesar

Smith, B. (2012, May 10). Pukekaikiore. Retrieved March, 2023, from http://barrysinparadise.blogspot.com/2012/05/pukekaikiore.html

Smithsonian Magazine. (2021, September 22). Genetic study maps when and how Polynesians settled the Pacific Islands. Retrieved March, 2023, from https://www.smithsonianmag.com/science-nature/genetic-study-maps-when-and-how-polynesians-settled-the-pacific-islands-180978733/

Stade, K. (2020). The first meeting - Abel Tasman and Māori in Golden Bay / Mohua. Retrieved March, 2023, from http://www.theprow.org.nz/events/the-first-meeting-abel-tasman-and-maori-in-golden-bay/

Stone, K. J. (2017, March 30). Archives and Special Collections. Retrieved March, 2023, from https://blogs.unimelb.edu.au/librarycollections/2017/03/30/staten-landt-where-the-americas-meet-the-antipodes/

Strom, C. (2018, December 30). The Māori: A rich and cherished culture at the world's edge. Retrieved March, 2023, from https://www.ancient-origins.net/history-famous-people/maori-0011250

Te Ruapekapeka Trust and Department of Conservation. (2014, January 1). The "Musket Wars". Retrieved March, 2023, from https://www.ruapekapeka.co.nz/maori-warfare/the-musket-wars/

Twinkl. (2023). Papatūānuku and Ranginui. Retrieved March, 2023, from https://www.twinkl.ca/teaching-wiki/papatuanuku-and-ranginui

The University of Waikato Te Whare Wānanga o Waikato. (2017). Our New Zealand dinosaur fossils. Retrieved March, 2023, from https://www.sciencelearn.org.nz/events/18-our-new-zealand-dinosaur-fossils

Victoria University of Wellington Library. (2016). Retrieved from https://nzetc.victoria.ac.nz/tm/scholarly/tei-Bea04Cook-t1-body-d23.html

Victoria University of Wellington. (2016). Māori and Polynesian: Their origin, history and culture. Retrieved March, 2023, from https://nzetc.victoria.ac.nz/tm/scholarly/tei-BroMaor-t1-body1-d4-d7.html

Villiers, Alan John. (2023, February 10). James Cook. Retrieved March, 2023, from https://www.britannica.com/biography/James-Cook

Wallis, Helen Margaret. (2022, April 25). Abel Tasman. Retrieved March, 2023, from https://www.britannica.com/biography/Abel-Tasman

Walrond, C. (2017, July 15). Gold and gold mining. Retrieved March, 2023, from https://teara.govt.nz/en/gold-and-gold-mining

Weir, B. (2017, November 13). The worst place on earth to be a predatory mammal. Retrieved March, 2023, from https://www.cnn.com/travel/article/wonder-list-bill-weir-new-zealand-predator-free-2050/index.html

Whitmore, R. (2008). The discovery of New Zealand. Retrieved March, 2023, from http://history-nz.org/discovery5.html

Wilson, J. (2022, April 20). European discovery of New Zealand. Retrieved March, 2023, from https://teara.govt.nz/en/european-discovery-of-new-zealand

Yarwood, V. (March-April 2005). Abel Tasman. New Zealand Geographic, (072).

Made in the USA
Las Vegas, NV
20 December 2024

14903181R00069